Prayer
50th Anniversary Edition

Books by Karl Barth
published by Westminster John Knox Press

Prayer

50th Anniversary Edition

Karl Barth

Edited by Don E. Saliers

From the translation of Sara F. Terrien

With Essays by

I. John Hesselink, Daniel L. Migliore,
and Donald K. McKim

Westminster John Knox Press
LOUISVILLE • LONDON

Cover design by Pam Poll Graphic Design

Published by Westminster John Knox Press
Louisville, Kentucky

This book is printed on acid-free paper that meets the American National Standards Institute Z39.48 standard. ∞

PRINTED IN THE UNITED STATES OF AMERICA

02 03 04 05 06 07 08 09 10 11 — 10 9 8 7 6 5 4 3 2 1

Cataloging-in-Publication Data can be obtained from the Library of Congress.

ISBN 0-664-22421-0

Contents

Publisher's Notes

To Anniversary Edition, 2002

Prayer, 50th Anniversary Edition is a new presentation of Barth's *Prayer, Second Edition*, published in 1985 by Westminster Press. This Anniversary Edition celebrates the 50th anniversary of Sara Terrien's translation, published by Westminster Press in 1952 as Karl Barth, *Prayer According to the Catechisms of the Reformation*.

This new volume maintains the fine Introduction and update to this work by Don E. Saliers from the 1985 edition and a selection of Barth's pastoral prayers. It also adds three essays by scholars of Barth's thought to provide a fuller picture of Barth's overall views on prayer, and particularly the Lord's Prayer, on which he focuses in the lectures presented here.

To Karl Barth, *Prayer, Second Edition*, 1985

The French original of this work was created by the Reverend André Perret under the supervision of A. Roulin from a shorthand transcription of seminars given by Barth at Neuchâtel between 1947 and 1949. The present edition of the text updates the translation of Sara F. Terrien to reflect changes of usage which have taken place since it was first published but which, often surprisingly, bear us back with greater fidelity to the breadth of Barth's theological thought and human sensitivity. The exemplary pastoral prayers, here added to enhance the usefulness of the book to its audience, are similarly edited from the translation by Keith R. Crim.

Prayer and Theology
in Karl Barth

From the very beginning the Lord's Prayer has occupied a place of singular honor in the life and liturgy of Christian churches. It has been central to the formation of faith in every generation and has been interpreted to the faithful and to their children's children by numberless teachers and theologians. Karl Barth's lectures on the Lord's Prayer thus stand in a tradition of teaching and interpretation stretching back to the apostles and the authors of the Gospels, as well as to the first evangelization of the churches, both Jewish and Gentile. This tradition of interpretation, first occurring in the Gospels of Luke and Matthew, has taken the Lord's Prayer as a model and as a touchstone to the nature of all Christian prayer, and Barth is no exception to it.

For Barth, like the Reformers he seeks to interpret, and like all great teachers of the Christian faith, prayer is the heart of the matter. He refers to the Reformation itself as "an act of continuous prayer, an invocation." There can be no human knowledge of God and no theological knowledge of our humanity apart from the sustained act of prayer. Whatever else is said of the monumental legacy bequeathed to the world by Barth's life and work, this must be emphasized: his theology and his life manifest what it means to "begin and end in prayer."

In these lectures, first delivered in French nearly forty years ago, we gain fresh access to the heart of Barth's theological enterprise. In them he is at his most Reformed, yet most ecumenical; most focused, yet most wide-ranging; most concerned with careful exegesis, yet most spontaneous and salty. And we can still catch his own delight in discovering and developing ideas orally. But this text is not to be read simply as the pastoral application of doctrines already nailed down. These pages reveal theological investigation in its most lively form. Because Barth's lines are so winsome and accessible, their implications for the doctrine of God and the Christian life are all the greater.

While Barth's discourses have been considered by some to present his "theology of prayer," I wish to invite a different reading. He is not so much engaged in applying a theology to prayer (as one might apply a theory to a particular case) as in giving us a theology in the making. In other words, while Barth addresses the Lord's Prayer in the context of the catechisms of the Reformation, the intent of his thought is to produce a prayer-oriented, or even liturgical, theology. As G. W. Bromiley has recently suggested, there is in Barth "the ultimate orienting of theology to worship." * His own pastoral prayers, a selection of which are included following the text, are worthy of study not only because they show an exemplary piety (though Barth was disquieted by the thought of published prayers) but because they are theological explorations of the church at prayer.

It is helpful to note at the outset the context in which Barth's reflections are embedded. He patterns his discus-

---

*G. W. Bromiley, *Introduction to the Theology of Karl Barth* (Eerdmans, 1979), 249.

sion of the topic of prayer and the petitions of the Lord's Prayer after the Reformers, specifically Calvin, Luther, and the Heidelberg Catechism. Thus the voices of Luther and Calvin are heard, at times quite distinctly. Yet, as is characteristic of the *Church Dogmatics* and other of Barth's writings, we often see both Luther and Calvin used as a stereoscope, as it were. That is, Barth often places them side by side in order to look through both to a deeper, multidimensional picture of the meaning and reality of Christian prayer. Barth gently suggests their limitations as well, as we shall note later concerning eschatology.

Luther and Calvin weave a rich tapestry of references to the Lord's Prayer into the whole of their theological writings. Luther frequently refers to it in his sermons and short catechetical pieces, most charmingly perhaps in his "Simple Instructions for Prayer" to Peter the barber at Wittenberg. Calvin as well makes use of the Lord's Prayer in teaching and preaching, but with particular force and breadth in chapter twenty of Book III of his *Institutes of the Christian Religion*. There, as in the catechetical situations of teaching in the churches at Wittenberg, Geneva, and elsewhere, an exposition of the Lord's Prayer is found in the context of considering the human dimensions of a prayerful life—its conditions, discipline, and vicissitudes.

Calvin and Luther themselves stand in a long tradition of exegesis and interpretation of the Lord's Prayer. So when Barth speaks of the first three petitions as dealing with the glory of God, he is echoing not only the specific accents of Calvin but also a tradition as ancient as Tertullian and Cyprian. The early fathers of the church regarded the Lord's Prayer as part of the very mystery of baptism into Christ. As we know from a study of early rites of initiation, the "handing over" of the prayer to new converts was part of the specific Christian identification of prayer for the newly baptized. Postbaptismal instruction thus often included drawing implications for the whole spiritual life from the privilege of being able to pray the Lord's Prayer with new understanding.

But it is significant that the early fathers of the church also regarded the Lord's Prayer as prayer at its highest. In the West, the early treatises of Tertullian and Cyprian laid the foundations for subsequent catechetical and exegetical approaches. In Alexandria the brilliant Origen, followed by such figures as Theodore of Mopsuestia and Gregory of Nyssa, contributed a decidedly speculative and mystical strand to the unfolding history of interpretation of the prayer. Each of the major early treatises or catechetical homilies, including those of Augustine at the end of the fifth century, reflects upon various features of Christian prayer, theological and practical, in the course of expositing the Lord's Prayer. This is vividly present in Barth's approach as well.

Thus we touch upon an extraordinarily rich tradition which views the Lord's Prayer both as Scripture—the Word of God to be exegeted—and as a model and rule of Christian prayer and life. Not only is this Christ's own teaching and rule, but it involves understanding the way of life he gives to those who use this prayer.

When Barth moves us into the inner life of the Lord's Prayer, he is both eliciting our faith response to the teaching and rule of Christian prayer from Jesus and expressing theological insight into who Jesus Christ is, hence who the triune God is, and hence who we are in living relation with God. We read Barth's exposition most faithfully when the presence of this hidden tradition is understood. It is theology close to life.

The distinctive emphases of Luther and Calvin are brought out in Barth's initial observations. For Luther, prayer is fundamentally obedience to the command of God. For Calvin the accent falls upon the continuing intercession of Jesus Christ. We address ourselves to God through the only Mediator, animated by his Holy Spirit. This difference is strikingly evident in the pattern of the Reformers' catechisms: For Luther, the Ten Commandments are always first, followed by the Creed and the Lord's Prayer. For Calvin, first the Creed, signifying our baptism into Christ's mediation, then the Commandments and the life of prayer. Luther is characteristically in combat, Calvin in reverential fear and the discipline of the Christian life. Calvin's influence may be seen especially in Barth's stress on the world as the theater for God's glory. To make God's name holy on earth as it is in heaven is to acknowledge the divine handiwork and to intend the visible world as the bearer of the name of the Creator. But Luther's heightened awareness of the abuses and even idolatries of prayer shows through in Barth's insistence that prayer must be both heartfelt and understood if it is to be true to the command. Such differences are more "tonal" than substantial by the time Barth is finished pointing to the deeper insights shared by both. That point may be best left to the judgment of the reader.

Some particular features of Barth's approach invite comment. There is something in these remarks which reminds us of Augustine's *Confessions*. Barth will suddenly and without warning be overheard addressing God. His transitions from prose exposition and argumentation to the language of address cannot be predicted. The movement in and out of an indicative account to the vocative of address also reminds us of Paul's letters. One might observe this precedent and note also what it is that prompts the explicit doxology: In pattern and tone these doxological passages are often reminiscent of eucharistic prayers, especially the patristic and recently revised prayers of thanksgiving. Occasionally we are startled by a vigorous prayer against misunderstanding, such as against flippancy and superficial biblicism (see page 34). Such features make Barth's lectures catechetical in more than one sense. The salty "semper reformanda" (always in need of reformation) is at work!

One is immediately invited to ponder the inner essence of Christian prayer as solidarity with all humanity. To pray the Lord's Prayer, and to pray with the church, is to address God through Jesus on behalf of humanity. This insight into the vocation of all baptized Christians is especially borne out in what Barth says in the *Church Dogmatics* about baptism as prayer and the ministry of the church.* This fundamental point recurs in the *Evangelical Theology* as well.†

Structurally, Barth follows Calvin over Luther in dividing the Lord's Prayer into six rather than seven petitions. Thus, "lead us not into temptation, but deliver us from evil" is treated as one cry for complex deliverance. Luther's particular struggle and turmoil with the Devil and with evil forces is brought out in a separate reflection. It is clear, however, that with both Calvin and Luther, Barth sees the whole prayer as an invitation from God for us to participate in the rule and reign of God's life and kingdom, both here and now and in the life to come. This is part of God's desire for us not to be alone. So there is no invidious distinction between "public" and "private"

Church Dogmatics, IV/3, sec. 74, 4.
†*Evangelical Theology: An Introduction*, trans. Grover Foley (Holt, Rinehart & Winston, 1963).

prayer for Barth. One may and must pray alone, but it is always the church at prayer, whether we are alone or assembled. Likewise, to pray is to stand before God in our own humanity, whether we are together or by ourselves.

While Barth is careful to mark differences between the Reformers at various particular points, his essential achievement is to give us a *synoptic* view. This is certainly not to be confused with a *synthetic* view which attempts to yoke them into some artificial unity. But one need not read very far into the Introductory Remarks or the exposition of the Lord's Prayer itself to discern Barth's drive toward a living synthesis of the Reformers' theological preoccupations. The daring aspect of Barth's treatment is found in his acute awareness of the twentieth-century context in which Christians struggle to pray and to understand once again the wellsprings of the great catechetical traditions.

Barth is not unaware of the problems of patriarchal exclusivism in the Lord's Prayer, though he certainly does not make this an explicit theme. The very phrase "Our Father" is not a natural patriarchal concept applied to God. Rather, as a term it emerges in the concrete relationship between the fullness of God and Jesus Christ. It means, he says, "Our Father of mercy" (p. 24). The notion of divine Fatherhood is not to be a projection from a previously held stereotype or cultural concept. It can only assume its true meaning when we find ourselves children, sisters and brothers of Christ, those whom Barth describes as "prodigal sons [and daughters]." Humanity, Barth observes, may behave "as a naughty child who cries and scolds its mother. But its mother is there."

Perhaps the most forceful departure from the Reformers, despite his gentle phrase "slightly corrected version," has to do with eschatology. Here it is obvious that

Barth wishes to claim that all Christian prayer is radically eschatological. This is seen in his interpretation of the whole context of the Lord's Prayer. The Word of promise of what God has done and is yet to accomplish in the created orders—"on earth as in heaven"—permeates the whole prayer. This note is sounded in each petition, but especially in the last. There is the great temptation, "the eschatological temptation," the absolute evil which threatens us with oblivion and nothingness. The whole of the prayer must be understood as being prayed with Jesus against all that opposes God.

The eschatological understanding of the whole prayer is linked with Barth's fundamental conviction that God is faithful to God's self-given Word: the kingdom and the power and the glory are finally, in Christ Jesus, God's alone. This means that prayer is an eschatological cry based precisely on the acknowledgment of God's name, will, and reign. All the particulars of our real and actual needs with which we petition God are themselves signs of our yearning for that which has yet to come on earth. As Barth remarks elsewhere, "Prayer is the actualization of our eschatological reality that is possible here and now. Because we actualize our eschatological reality in prayer, ... to be living in Christ, Christian prayer must say finally, 'Not my will but thy will be done.'"*

A final set of observations about the relation between prayer and the doctrine of God may assist us in appreciating how skillful Barth is in doing theology as exposition of the Lord's Prayer. Among recent theologians, few have captured as profoundly the patristic conception of the inner connection between the act of prayer and theologi-

---

Ethics, ed. Dietrich Braun; trans. Geoffrey W. Bromiley (Seabury Press, 1981), 472–73.

cal reflection. A theology which begins, as Barth's does, with the actuality of God's self-disclosure and communication, places the reality of God's initiative and response at the center of Christian life and prayer. In fact, a case could be made that Barth's categories of the freedom and personal agency of God which are basic to any human communion with God are liturgical and not simply metaphysical or ontological. Prayer as the ongoing dialogue between Jesus Christ and the Father, hence between God and the people called out in promise, is worship as response through grace to the triune revelation of God. This basic insight can best be understood by examining what Barth says about prayer. That is why this slim text on the Reformers' catechisms and the Lord's Prayer is of a piece with his more formal theological work.

In his *Evangelical Theology: An Introduction*, Barth makes four basic claims which form the hermeneutic, so to speak, of this intrinsic relation between the vocative of prayer and the indicative of theology. "The first and basic act of theological work is prayer."* This sounds a theme heard in the whole sweep of the *Church Dogmatics*. Theology itself, while demanding historical knowledge and conceptual reasoning, is radically dependent upon having been addressed by God in such a manner as to respond freely in return. Theological work, Barth claims, "does not merely begin with prayer and is not merely accompanied by it; in its totality it is peculiar and characteristic of theology that it can be performed only in the act of prayer."† The articulation of a doctrine of God is not simply motivated by prayer; it is pervaded by it. The conception of God must be congruent with the nature of address

*Evangelical Theology: An Introduction, p. 160.
†Ibid.

to the self-revealing God, whose revelation is accompanied by the command and invitation to share the divine
life.

This is the essential unity between prayer and theological endeavor, according to Barth. Thinking about God
and speaking the truth of the gospel are possible insofar as
they emerge from addressing God faithfully. The whole
subject of "God in Christ reconciling the world" must
illuminate every topic in theology and display a unity,
necessity, and beauty which is grounded in prayer to God.
This recognizes, of course, the limits of human effort to
reason to God from the world of human experience; but
it also specifies the "object" of faith and the ground of
prayer. The essence of prayer and worship, then, is
acknowledgment of God and God's gracious turning in
mercy and judgment toward all creation. This response
arises from the capacity of the creature, through grace, to
love and to rejoice in gratitude for who God is. This, it
seems to me, is precisely what emerges in Barth's treatment of the Lord's Prayer, both in its order of petition and
in its expression of real human needs and acknowledgment before God.

The second claim is that the object of theological
reflection is a "Thou" encountered, not an idea to be
grasped as the "Ultimate Good" or the "Ground of
Being," for instance. Doctrinal language about God must
be a response to something actually discerned in God. But
this means to thank, to praise, to invoke, and to petition
God. This is why Barth can say, "Theological work must
really and truly take place in the form of a liturgical act."*
This is implicit in Barth's reflection on the fact that we are
not only to speak the words Jesus gives us, but that we

*Ibid., 163.

must also receive him and the life of service which he confers in and through the words.

Thirdly, since theological reflection about God is itself dialogical, we cannot rest content with building upon the certainties of previous systems of thought. Rather it is a question of returning to God in prayer and worship, of "beginning once again at the beginning." To conceive God as living and redeeming the world is humanly possible only by our receiving anew through grace the present activity of God. Theology itself becomes an offering to God, and a continuous petition that this offering may be acceptable.

Finally, theology cannot guarantee truth, because it cannot in itself guarantee the grace of God. It must follow Anselm's prayer in the *Proslogion:* "Reveal thyself to me." Certainty in our knowledge of God lies not in formulated doctrines, according to Barth, but in acknowledging, invoking, and petitioning that God will truly make the divine Word and being accessible to us. This has fascinating ecclesial implications. For example, in his introductory remarks to our text Barth wryly observes: "Now if believers can pray together, they should also be able to take Communion together. For then doctrinal differences can only be of a secondary nature" (p. 5).

With these points in mind, we can appreciate the continuity of this lively set of lectures on the Reformers' concept of prayer in the catechisms. Barth's own intense understanding of the Lord's Prayer from the inside out, so to speak, unfolds a key aspect of his whole theological undertaking. While the task appears to be an informal exposition and posing of a "theology of prayer," it manifests the much more elemental feature of Barth's work, an entire theology oriented toward prayer and worship. In such a seemingly humble task as expositing the Lord's Prayer in the tradition of the church's exegetes and catechists, Barth has shown us both the inner logic of his enterprise and a recovery of a genuinely liturgical theology.

Don E. Saliers

St. John's Abbey
Institute for Cultural
*   and Ecumenical Research*
September 1984

Prayer

Introductory Remarks

B efore taking up the subject of prayer itself according to the catechisms of the Reformation, we believe it useful to present several observations which these texts have suggested to us.

1. The Reformers of the church prayed.

The Reformation appears to us as a great whole: a labor of research, thinking, preaching, discussion, polemic, and organization. But it was more than all that. From what we know, it was also an act of continuous prayer, an invocation, and, let us add, an act of human beings, of certain persons, and at the same time a response on the part of God.

We find in Luther's Large Catechism a remarkable passage from which we may cite a few excerpts:

> For we know that our defense lies in prayer alone.
> We are too weak to resist the Devil and his vassals.
> Let us hold fast to the weapons of the Christian; they
> enable us to combat the Devil. For what has carried
> off these great victories over the undertakings of our

enemies which the Devil has used to put us in sub-
jection, if not the prayers of certain pious people
who rose up as a rampart to protect us? Our enemies
may mock at us. But we shall oppose both them and
the Devil if we maintain ourselves in prayer and if we
persist in it. For we know that when a Christian
prays in this way: "Dear Father, thy will be done,"
God replies, "Dear child, yes, it shall be done in spite
of the Devil and of the whole world."

There are some mysteries in the events of the sixteenth
century, but here we touch upon a point of particular
importance. Perhaps the faults and weaknesses that we see
at some moments in history are due to the fact that we no
longer understand the meaning of words such as these we
have just heard from Luther.

2. The Reformers were of one mind concerning the importance and significance of prayer.

When the texts of the various catechisms are read and
compared, it is possible to distinguish with some clarity
the dominant preoccupations of Calvin, Luther, and the
authors of the Heidelberg Catechism.

However, it would be difficult, even impossible, to dis-
cover contradictions on the matter of faith. One of these
men, for example, insists that prayer is obedience to a
command of God: human beings must pray because God
wills it. One might suppose that this comes from Calvin.
But it is Luther who holds this rigid, almost military idea:
God commands, we must obey. Another insists that
prayer is founded upon the intercession of Jesus Christ
with his heavenly Father. One might expect this to come
from Luther, but it is from Calvin.

Furthermore, Calvin insists upon the necessity of believers addressing themselves to God alone, rather than to the saints or to the angels. We recognize again the Genevan Reformer when he speaks of the part played by the Holy Spirit in prayer. On the other hand, it is interesting to note that prayer is mentioned as an act of gratitude in the Heidelberg Catechism.

Let us also observe that the example and the reality of prayer are identical in all these texts. This fact should be understood in the discussions which persist even today in Germany between Lutherans and Calvinists. Inasmuch as the Reformers were of one mind concerning prayer, they were in fundamental agreement. Now, if believers can pray together, they should also be able to take Communion together. For then doctrinal differences can be only of a secondary nature.

3. What is not to be found in these texts

One fact needs to be stressed: these texts do not mention any differences between individual prayer and corporate prayer. For the authors of the various catechisms one thing is clear: they see the church, *us*, that is to say, the members of a community forming a whole. But they distinguish also among the individuals who constitute this whole. One cannot ask whether it is the Christians who pray, or the church. There is no alternative, for when the Christians pray, it is the church; and when the church prays, it is the Christians. Between these two there can be no opposition.

Perhaps it is a sign of sickness in the church that questions such as these can arise: How can I, in my room, pray for my spiritual needs? And the church, on its side, how can it pray? Thereupon, one begins to take a peculiar

interest in prayer within the church and thus in the "liturgical question"! Is this not the sign of a disease?

For the Reformers there is no "liturgical question": one
prays in the church or one prays at home. They are not
preoccupied with drawing a distinction between private
and communal prayer. What interests them is the necessity to pray and to pray well. There is here perhaps a warning and a reminder. Any stress on secondary matters
reveals a spiritual weakness.

4. Another question overlooked in these texts: Must one pray from the heart, or according to a formulary?

Neither Calvin nor Luther paid heed to this question
which preoccupies so many of our contemporaries. They
insisted that it is from the heart that one must pray. They
emphasized sincerity of prayer in opposition to the mum-
bling of lips. They knew what free prayer is, but they also
knew that true prayer cannot be a matter of fantasy; it
must be disciplined.

Jesus Christ not only told us to pray, but he also showed
us in the "Our Father" how we are to pray. We should do
well to hold fast to this rule. There must be affection in
prayer, as Calvin says, but this affection may not be for our
minds a pretext of vagabondage. The extemporaneous
prayers that Calvin used to make at the end of his sermons
are remarkable in their majestic uniformity. He did not
permit himself disorderly effusions. The same elements
always reappear: adoration of the majesty of God and of
the Holy Spirit; but they are not clichés.

The Reformers were not glib at prayer, and I do not
know whether they would willingly have spoken of the gift
of prayer. They say: Pray and pray well; this is what matters. Be content with possessing in the Lord's Prayer a

model, but let your prayer arise from the freedom of the heart.

5. The Reformers do not speak of a difference between explicit prayer (which is exteriorized, at certain times, by the enunciation of words) and implicit prayer (which is not expressed in words but lies in sentiments, in a continuous attitude of heart, conscience, and thought).

The "pray constantly" of 1 Thessalonians 5:17 is not quoted in any catechism of that period. It would seem that the chief preoccupation of these authors is explicit prayer. However, Calvin says that language is not always necessary. In a general way, it may be stated that according to the explanations of the Reformers themselves—that is, what they say in their writings, their preaching, and their actions—prayer is at once word, thought, and life.

Chapter 1

Prayer

We shall examine the subject in three of its aspects: first, the problem of prayer in general; then, prayer viewed as a gift of God; and finally, prayer considered as a human act.

1. The problem of prayer

In these catechisms what importance is given to prayer? If you glance over them, you will notice that Luther treated first the Commandments, then the Creed, that is, the exposition of faith. Calvin, on the other hand, began with the Creed and then turned to the Commandments. Thus he speaks of faith first and then of obedience.

Here we are, then, we Christians, looked upon as believers, as obedient servants, and as such faced with a new problem: that of prayer. Is it really a new problem? beyond faith and obedience? So it would seem. Calvin says that prayer deals with our life and our relation to the exigencies of this world. The question is as follows: I, who am a Christian, can I really live according to the word of the gospel and of the law, according to my faith and in obedience? Shall I be able to live thus in the midst of the necessities of my existence?—Yes, according to the gospel it is possible in the holiness of obedience to live that which is given us to live, that which we must live. In order to do this, we must listen to what is told us about prayer and ask God himself to come to our aid, to instruct us, to give us the possibility of walking in this path. Such a quest must be made in order that we may live. Prayer is this quest.

In Luther's Catechism, this situation of human beings grappling with faith and obedience is closely examined. What is to be said, what is to be done, when we are confronted with the fact that no one obeys the law perfectly, whereas the law exacts perfect obedience, and when we do not perfectly fulfill it, we do not fulfill it at all? However, we are believers, that is, people who have the beginnings of faith. Faith is not something we carry about in our pockets as a rightful possession. God says to me, "Put your trust in me, believe in me." And I go forward, I believe; but while going forward, I say, "Come to the help of mine unbelief." Life is there before us with its difficulties and its demands; and the law is also there to claim obedience in spite of our weaknesses, and so are the obstacles which rise up before us. I go forward with a faith that is only a poor beginning, and I am commanded to go ahead, to become perfectly obedient, to continue on this path of faith after I have already taken the first step.

On the one hand, there is our inward life, that of weak and wily human beings. On the other hand, there is our outward life in this world, with all its enigmas and difficulties. There is also the judgment of God, who encounters us and says to us at every moment, "This is not enough." I may even reach the point of asking myself, "Underneath it all, am I a Christian? My faith being small and my obedience slight, of what meaning are these words: 'I believe, I obey'?" Deep is the abyss. The core of our being is put to question at the very moment we believe and obey as well as we can. In this situation (which is the same for every Christian) prayer means going toward God, asking him to give us what we lack—strength, courage, serenity, prudence—asking him to teach us how to obey the law and accomplish the commandments, and then that God may instruct us how to continue in believing and believing yet more, and that he may renew our faith.

Such a request can be made solely to God. As Calvin has said, it is a question of honor which we owe to his divinity. It is an honor due to him who has revealed himself to us by his Word (thus the Heidelberg Catechism). For it is the word of God that maintains us in this situation wherein prayer becomes a necessity.

Prayer means that we address ourselves to God, who has already spoken to us in the gospel and in the law. We find ourselves face to face with him when we are tormented by the imperfection of our obedience and the discontinuity of our faith. Because of God we are in distress. God alone is able to heal us of it. In order to ask him to do so, we pray.

Calvin points out that we are not alone in this difficult position. We have sisters and brothers in Christ, and from them we may also receive guidance and encouragement. Yet it is only a ministry, a dispensation of the wealth of God, that human beings can bring to the misery of our situation. God himself bestows upon them an honor when he uses them to communicate his benefits to us, and thereby he obligates us to them. Prayer cannot therefore in any way estrange us from other people; it can only unite us since it involves a matter that concerns us all.

Before praying, then, I first seek the company of others. I know that all of you are facing the same difficulties as I. Let us therefore consult with one another and mutually give what we are able. However, we cannot put our trust in fellow creatures. There may be a few capable of telling us what we need, or at least of giving us certain indications. But the gift itself can come from God alone. We cannot pray to fellow humans, no more to the saints than to the others.

In the sixteenth century it was important to say that the saints of the church, or any of the dead, are unable to help us. Perhaps, however, such a categorical statement might be questioned. I am not so sure that the saints of the church are unable to come to our aid. I mean the Reformers, for example, and the saints who are alive on earth today. We live in communion with the church of the past, and from it we receive help. Yet, one fact is certain: that neither the living nor the dead can be for us what God is to us, namely, a help in that great distress which is ours in the face of the gospel and the law. The same thing may be said in respect to the angels, who can help us but cannot be invoked.

Thus for the Reformers everything was reduced to this question: How is it possible for me to have an encounter with God? I have heard his word, I wish sincerely to listen to it, and yet here I am in my insufficiency. The Reformers were not unaware of other difficulties, but they knew that such hindrances are all implicit in the following reality: I stand before God with my desires, my thoughts, my misery; I must live with him, for to live means nothing other than to live with God. Here I am, caught between the exigencies of life, both small and great, and the necessity of prayer. The Reformers tell us the first thing is to pray.

2. Prayer as a gift of God

Prayer is a grace, an offer of God.

We shall not begin, as the Reformers did, with a description of what we do when we pray. Obviously we do something, we act; to understand this action, however, we must begin with the end, that is, we must first consider the answer to prayer. We may be surprised at this, for, from a logical standpoint, we should ask first, "What is prayer?" And only afterward, "Do we receive an answer when we pray?" Now for the Reformers the basic and vital point is this certitude: God does answer prayer. That is the first thing we must know. Calvin says it explicitly: We obtain what we request. Prayer is grounded upon this assurance.

Let us approach the subject from the given fact that God answers. God is not deaf, but listens; more than that, he acts. God does not act in the same way whether we pray or not. Prayer exerts an influence upon God's action, even upon his existence. This is what the word "answer" means.

In Question 129 of the Heidelberg Catechism it is stated that the answer to our prayer is more certain than our awareness of the things that we request. It seems there is nothing more sure than the feeling of our desires, but this Catechism says that God's answer is still more certain. We too must have this inward assurance. Perhaps we doubt the sincerity of our prayer and the worth of our request. But one thing is beyond doubt: it is the answer that God gives. Our prayers are weak and poor. Nevertheless, what matters is not that our prayers be forceful, but that God listens to them. That is why we pray.

How does God answer us? Here we must recall the article on Jesus Christ in Calvin's Catechism. We cannot better understand God's answer than by keeping in mind this thought: Jesus Christ is our brother, we belong to him; he is the head of the body of which we are the members; and at the same time he is the Son of God, of God himself. It is he who has been given to us as mediator and advocate before God. We are not separated from God, and more important still, God is not separated from us. We may be without God, but God is not without humankind. This we must know, and this is what matters. Facing the godless, there is God, who is never without us, because humanity—all of us—is in the presence of God. If God knows humanity, if he sees us and judges us, it is always through the person of Jesus Christ, his own Son, who has been obedient and is the object of his delight. By Jesus Christ, humanity is in the presence of God. God looks at Christ, and it is through him that he looks at us. We have, therefore, a representative before God.

Calvin even says that we pray through the mouth of Jesus Christ, who speaks for us because of what he has been, because of what he has suffered in obedience and faithfulness to his Father. And we ourselves pray as though with his mouth, inasmuch as he gives us access and audience, and intercedes for us. Thus, fundamentally, our prayer is already made even before we formulate it. When we pray, we can only return to that prayer which was uttered in the person of Jesus Christ and which is constantly repeated because God is not without humankind.

God is the Father of Jesus Christ, and that very man Jesus Christ has prayed, and he is praying still. Such is the foundation of our prayer in Jesus Christ. It is as if God himself has pledged to answer our request because all our prayers are summed up in Jesus Christ; God cannot fail to answer, since it is Jesus Christ who prays.

The fact that God yields to human petitions, that he alters his intentions and follows the bent of our prayers, is not a sign of weakness. In his own majesty and in the splendor of his might, he has willed and yet wills it so. He desires to be the God who has been made flesh in Jesus Christ. Therein lies his glory, his omnipotence. He does not then impair himself by yielding to our prayer; on the contrary, it is in so doing that he shows his greatness.

If God himself wishes to enter into fellowship with humankind and be close to us as a father is to his child, he does not thereby weaken his might. God cannot be greater than he is in Jesus Christ. If God answers our prayer, it is not then only because he listens to us and increases our faith (the efficacy of prayer has sometimes been explained in this manner), but because he is God: Father, Son, and Holy Spirit, God whose word has been made flesh.

Let us now come back to Luther, who invites us, nay, who commands us, to pray. If we do not pray, we fail to realize that we are in the presence of God. We cannot recognize what he is. Such an attitude would render us incapable of grasping the fact that God meets us in Jesus Christ. Now, when we are aware of this mystery, we must pray. Jesus Christ is there—he, the Son of God; and we who belong to him—we, for whom there is no other possibility than to follow him, to speak through his mouth— are with him. We have found the right road, and now it behooves us to walk in it. On this path, the gospel and the law, the promise and the commandments of God, are one and the same thing. God opens this road to us; he commands us to pray. Thus it is not possible to say "I shall pray" or "I shall not pray," as if it were an act according to our own good pleasure. To be a Christian and to pray are one and the same thing; it is a matter that cannot be left to our caprice. It is a need, a kind of breathing necessary to life.

The Heidelberg Catechism is still more precise. It affirms that prayer is quite simply the first act of thanksgiving toward

God. The word "thanksgiving"* is more appropriate than gratitude because it means acting according to what we know has been given. Every one of us who knows God must return thanks to him. We recognize what God is, what God has done for us in Jesus Christ; we enter into the condition that has been given us in Christ. And in this condition we pray.

Luther even adds that God would be angered if we did not pray, for we should be despising the gift that he has bestowed on us. Since it is God himself who tells us to pray, how could we neglect to do so? The Reformers remind us that prayer is not a matter of convenience; it is, in the life of a Christian, a necessary and essential act, which must come by itself.

Furthermore, God, since he is our God, causes our prayer to proceed from his grace. Wherever there is the grace of God, human beings pray. God works in us, for we know not how to pray as we ought. It is the Spirit of God that incites us and enables us to pray in a fitting manner. We are not skilled to judge whether we are worthy or capable of praying, or whether we have sufficient zeal to pray. Grace in itself is the answer to this question. When we are comforted by the grace of God, we begin to pray with or without words.

God also points out a way that will lead us to prayer. Prayer is neither an arbitrary act nor a step to be taken blindly. When we pray, we cannot venture according to whim in this or that direction, with just any sort of request. For God commands us to follow him and to take

----

*[Translator's Note] This is a paraphrase [sometimes rendered "acknowl-edgement"] of the author's use of the French word *reconnaissance*, which cannot be accurately rendered in English: "*Le mot de reconnaissance est plus clair que celui de gratitude, car il signifie: agir selon ce que nous connaissons (reconnaître). Tout homme qui connait Dieu doit être reconnaissant envers lui. Il reconnaît ce que Dieu est, ce qu'il a fait pour lui en Jésus-Christ; il entre dans la position qui nous est donnée en Christ; et dans cette position, l'homme prie.*"

the place that he has assigned to us. It is a matter ruled by God, not by our own initiative.

How shall we pray? It was not by chance that Jesus gave us a formulary in the Lord's Prayer to instruct all human beings how to pray aright. God himself teaches us how we are to pray, for we have so many things to ask! And we think that what we desire is always so important! Besides, it is necessary for us to believe this. But in order that our act may become true prayer, we must accept the offer that God tenders us. We cannot pray by ourselves, and if we have deceptions in prayer, we must accept God's showing us the way of true prayer. He therefore starts us, with all our needs and problems, on a certain path by which we can bring everything to him; but we must take that path. This discipline is necessary for us. If it is absent, we must not be surprised that we cry out in a void, instead of finding ourselves engaged in a prayer that has already been heard.

Let us be content with possessing this formula of the Lord's Prayer, as the Reformers say, so that in praying thus we may serve our apprenticeship in true prayer. Calvin justly declares that in prayer also we cannot act as strangers, but as citizens of the City of God we must accept its constitution, its law, and its order. Only under this condition can we expect a hearing and a reply to the problems of our life.

Because he is our God in Jesus Christ, God himself compels us to take in his presence an attitude that at first sight appears to be rash and bold. He obliges us to meet him with a certain audacity: "Thou hast made us promises, thou hast commanded us to pray; and here I am, coming, not with pious ideas or because I like to pray (perhaps I do not like to pray), and I say to thee what thou hast commanded me to say, 'Help me in the necessities of my life.' Thou must do so; I am here." Luther is right: the position of one at prayer requires utter humility as well as an attitude of boldness. There is a good kind of humility; it consists in accepting, through liberty, this place that we have in Jesus vis-à-vis God. If we are sure of our attitude, and if we do not come to God merely on account of our good intentions, then this liberty is self-evident.

Thus God's will in our favor and his mercy in Jesus are decisive elements in the matter now at hand. The Heidelberg Catechism, in Question 117, affirms that our sure foundation rests on the fact that, because of Jesus Christ, God can answer our prayer in spite of our unworthiness.

3. Prayer as a human act

According to the foregoing considerations, prayer is an altogether simple act by which we accept and use the divine offer; an act in which we obey this command of the majestic grace that identifies itself with the will of God. To obey grace—to give thanks—means that prayer is also an act on the part of human beings, who know themselves to be sinners and call upon the grace of God. We find ourselves confronted by the gospel, the law, and the weakness of our faith, even if we are not conscious of it. We experience at once a certain sadness and a certain joy. But we have not yet understood that we are sinners or that we do not perfectly realize obedience. We do not yet know that we are under a veil. It must be removed. When we pray, our human condition is unveiled to us, and we know then that we are in this distress and also in that hope. It is God who places us in this situation; but at the same time he comes to our aid. Prayer is thus our human response when we understand our distress and know that help will come.

It is not permissible to consider prayer as a good work

to be done, as a pious, nice, and pretty duty to be performed. Prayer cannot be for us a means of creating something, of making a gift to God and to ourselves; we are in the position of persons who can only receive, who are obliged to speak now to God, since they have no one else whom they can address. Luther has said that we must all be destitute, for we are faced by a great void and have everything to receive and learn from God.

Prayer as a human act cannot be a gossiping, a series of phrases or mumblings. The Reformers insisted also on that point. They had in the Roman Church many examples of the sort of prayer against which they were fighting. The matter is simple and important for us too, even if we are not Roman Catholics: prayer must be an act of affection; it is more than a question of using the lips, for God asks the allegiance of our hearts. If the heart is not in it, if it is only a form which is carried out more or less correctly, what is it then? Nothing! All prayers offered solely by the lips are not only superfluous, but they are also displeasing to God; they are not only useless, but they are offensive to God. At this point it is also important to remark with Calvin that prayer uttered in a language that we do not understand or which the congregation at prayer does not understand is a mockery to God, a perverse hypocrisy, for the heart cannot be in it. We must think and speak in a comprehensible tongue, in a language which has meaning for us.

Let our prayer not be offered according to our good pleasure; otherwise there would be then on our part inordinate desires. Let it be patterned after the rule given by the One who knows our needs better than we ourselves. God has directed us first to submit ourselves to him in order that we may present our requests. So that we may conform to this order, we must eliminate in our prayers all questions like this: Does God listen to us? On this point Calvin is categorical: "Such a prayer is not a prayer." Doubt is not permitted, for it goes without saying that we shall be heard. Even before we pray we must assume the attitude of someone who has been heard.

We are not free to pray or not to pray, or to pray only when we feel so inclined, for prayer is not an act that comes naturally to us. It is a grace, and we can expect this grace only through the Holy Spirit. This grace is there, with God and his word in Jesus Christ. If we say yes to all that, if we receive what God gives, then everything is done, everything is settled, not on account of our good pleasure, but by the freedom we have in obeying him.

Above all, let us not begin by believing that humankind is passive, that we are in a sort of *farniente* ["do nothing"], in an armchair, and that we can say, "The Holy Spirit will pray for me." Never! Humankind is impelled to pray. We must do it. Prayer is an act, as well as a supplication to the Lord that he put us in this frame of mind which is agreeable to him. This is one of the facets of the problem of grace and liberty: we work but at the same time we very well know that God wills to fulfill our work; we are in this human liberty which is not crushed by the liberty of God; we allow the Holy Spirit to act, and yet, during this time, our mind and our heart do not sleep. Such is prayer when viewed as a human act.

Our participation in the work of God is the action that consists in giving our allegiance to this work. It is a great thing to preach, to believe, and to fulfill our small obedience to God's commandments. But in all these forms of obedience and faith it is prayer that puts us in rapport with God and permits us to collaborate with him. God wishes us to live with him, and we on our side reply, "Yes, Father, I wish to live with thee." And then he says, "Pray, call me; I am listening to you. I shall live and reign with you."

The Reformation was not made without these men named Calvin, Luther, and still others. God was laboring in allowing them to participate in his work. It was not by the brilliance of their virtues, wisdom, or piety that he accomplished his work with them. It was by prayer, at once humble and audacious. And it is in prayer thus understood that we are invited to participate, alone with God and in the community. This prayer is at once an act of humility and an act of triumph. Such an act is required of us because we are given the power to perform it.

Chapter 2

Interpreting the Lord's Prayer in the Tradition of the Reformers

The Invocation

We are invited to pray. That presupposes all we have said before on prayer in general. However, this is the important fact: we are exhorted to pray, "Our Father who art in heaven." It is Jesus Christ who invites us to address ourselves in prayer to God and to call him our Father; Jesus Christ, who is the Son of God, who has made himself our brother and makes us his brothers and sisters. He takes us with him in order to associate us with himself, to place us beside him so that we may live and act as his family and as the members of his body. He says to us, "Follow me."

The Lord's Prayer is not just any form of prayer to be used by just anybody. It presupposes "us": "Our Father"! It addresses a Father who is a father to us in a most particular fashion. This "us" is created by the order that Jesus gave to follow him. It implies the communion of all humanity praying with Jesus Christ, our existence in the fellowship of the children of God. Jesus Christ invites, permits, commands us to join him, especially in his intercession with God his Father. Jesus Christ invites us, commands us, and allows us to speak with him to God, to pray with him his own prayer, to be united with him in the Lord's Prayer. Therefore he invites us to adore God, pray to God, and praise God with one mouth and one soul, with him, united to him.

This "us" signifies also the communion of the one who prays with all those who are in his or her company and who are likewise invited to pray; with those who have received the same invitation, the same commandment, the same permission to pray beside Jesus Christ. We pray "Our Father" in the communion of this assembly, of this congregation which we call the church (if we take this expression in its original meaning of ecclesia, the congregation).

But even while we are in the communion of the saints, in the ecclesia of those who are brought together by Jesus Christ, we are also in communion with those who do not yet pray, perhaps, but for whom Jesus Christ prays, since he prays for humankind as a whole. It is the object of this intercession, and we ourselves enter into this communion with the whole of humanity. When Christians pray, they are, so to speak, the substitutes for all those who do not pray; and in this sense they are in communion with them in the same manner as Jesus Christ has entered into solidarity with sinners, with a lost human race.

"*Our Father,*" thou who hast begotten us, procreated us by thy Word, by thy Spirit; thou who art our Father because thou art our Creator, the Lord of the covenant which thou hast been pleased to make with humankind. Thou who hast begun in and with our creation and who art the end of our existence.

Our Father, thou who hast made thyself responsible for our whole existence, temporal and eternal; God the Father, thou whose glory is our heritage and to whom we have free access as children to their father. . .

Our Father, thou who by nature art ready simply to listen to us, to answer us. . . . But we forget it always.

We may deny God, but he cannot forget us, nor can he deny us. Being Father, he is faithful by nature. His superiority and his goodwill toward us are unchangeable.

This is what God is for us. But we must admit that we have no right to call him Father, to be his children, to address him in this manner. He is our Father, and we are his children by virtue of the natural relationship existing between him and Jesus Christ, by virtue of this Fatherhood and this Sonship which were made real in the person of Jesus Christ; and for us they are made real in him. We are his children, he is our Father, by virtue of this new birth realized at Christmas, on Good Friday, at Easter, and fulfilled at the moment of our baptism. It is a new birth, that is to say, a new existence, really new, a life quite different from the one that can be born of our human possibilities, of our own merits. "God our Father" means "Our Father of mercy." We are and always shall be prodigal sons who can claim no other right than that which is given us in the person of Jesus Christ.

This does not weaken what has been said of the divine Fatherhood. The clarity and the certitude, the very greatness and majesty of our Father appear in the fact that we find ourselves before him without power, without merit, without proper faith, and empty-handed. Yet in Christ we are the children of God. The reality of this sonship would not be more certain if there could be added to it anything whatsoever coming from us. The divine reality alone is the fullness of all reality.

Jesus Christ is the donor and the warrant of the divine Fatherhood and of our filiality. It is the reason for which this Fatherhood and this filiality are incomparably superior to any other, to any relationship suggested to us by the words "father," "son," "children." These human bonds are not the original, of which the other would be the image or symbol. The original, the true fatherhood, the true filiality are in these ties which God has created between himself and us. Everything which exists among us is merely the image of this original filiality. When we call God our Father, we do not fall into symbolism; on the contrary, we are in the full reality of these two words: "father" and "son."

"Who art in heaven." Heaven! It is a part of the created world, the portion which is above, the unapproachable and incomprehensible part of creation. This means: God, who is higher than heaven, who is beyond it, and who is also the Father of Jesus Christ, the one who loves the world in Jesus Christ. If one says of God, "He is limitless, incomprehensible, free, sovereign, eternal, omnipotent, transcendent," these expressions do not derive their exact meaning from an idea, from an abstraction, as if one wished to define the contrary of what is limited, comprehensible, and temporal. All these qualities draw their true meaning from the goodness of the heavenly Father, who has made himself our Father in Jesus Christ. Herein lies the meaning of his transcendence, of his existence beyond heaven. No philosophy, be it that of Aristotle, Kant, or Plato, can reach the transcendence of God, for the philosophers go only as far as the limits of the incomprehensible, of that which is superior to us. All philosophy turns around the subject of heaven. The gospel, on the other hand, speaks to us of him who is in heaven, beyond heaven. Neither the idealist nor the existentialist can bring us to the reality of God, to his transcendence, which is quite different from spirit, from invisibility. God's transcendence is demonstrated, revealed, and actualized in Jesus Christ, who is the profundity of his omnipotent mercy.

He is in heaven, on his throne. That is his supreme existence. He is there facing our desires, our needs great and small, our ideals and principles, our wisdom and our stupidity, our humanity and our animality. There is the Judge, the King who disposes of us, who sometimes rules against us, but in any case over us always. He is ever the same and yet never the same, because he is always new every morning. He is present with us at every instant, and he is eternal only by being present with us. He is free grace and gracious freedom, the person to whom all is submitted, all is entrusted, and in whose hands all can and must serve, have served, and will serve. He is, in a few words, the one whom we address not by our own initiative, but because we are invited, called, to do so. We have the freedom to come to him. This freedom is given to us; it is not of ourselves, it is not natural. It is the freedom of the children of God, the freedom of the Word and of the Spirit.

The Petitions of the Lord's Prayer

First let us attempt to consider the petitions as a whole. Let us notice that their order is, in a certain sense, analogous to that of the Ten Commandments. There is a clear difference between the first three and the last three. The first three correspond to the first four Commandments, and the last three to Commandments five through ten.

The first three petitions deal with the glory of God; there the Lord's Prayer begins. Thus we are permitted, even commanded, to take interest in God's cause, to pray that this cause of God—his name, his kingdom, his will—may be victorious, so that it may reach its fulfillment. In Jesus Christ, God has manifested himself as a God who, while being perfectly free and self-sufficient, yet does not wish to be alone. He does not wish to act, exist, live, labor, work, strive, vanquish, reign, and triumph without the human race. God does not wish, then, for his cause to be his alone; he wishes it to be ours as well.

Are there any real atheists, persons without God? In any case, even if there are human beings without God, there is, from the Christian viewpoint, no God without human beings. It is most important for us to understand this. God has been with us; he is with us: Emmanuel! He permits us, he commands us to pray, as we are invited to do in these first three requests, for the success of his cause. He invites us to participate in his work, in the government of the church, of the world. If we pray, "Hallowed be thy name. Thy kingdom come, thy will be done," we place ourselves at God's side, nothing less than that. God invites us to join his designs and his action. And let us note that this invitation comes at the beginning and is repeated at the end, in the doxology.

On these first three requests hang the freedom, the joy, the alacrity, and the certitude of the other petitions. All our entreaties presuppose that we ask to participate in God's cause. Whoever refused to do so would have no interest in this cause, nor would he know how to pray either for the forgiveness of his sins or for his daily bread; he would not understand what it is all about. We can live with God only when we are in agreement with his designs, with his cause, which includes ours and all the others. If not, it is as though we wished to stand in midair. We must have ground on which to walk, and in prayer we walk on the ground of these first three petitions. We must not be surprised that many prayers resound in a void and that they are neither listened to nor answered. However, all would be very simple if we understood that we must begin with the beginning and that we cannot pray in any other way.

The last three petitions concern us directly, with sharp actuality. It is a question of our comfort, our own good pleasure, our physical as well as spiritual and celestial salvation. Because in Jesus Christ God has united our cause (the major and the minor problems of our life) to his cause, we are permitted, nay commanded, to appeal now with simplicity on our behalf. And here all our life is at stake. It is not only a permission but an order to deposit with God and entrust to him all our baggage (for one arrives with a very complicated collection of baggage when one has traveled through this world). We can entrust to God this baggage, which is at once temporal, material, secular, eternal, Christian, ecclesiastical, and theological.

In Jesus Christ the human being is revealed. In him it becomes the creature par excellence *(kat' exochēn)*, which cannot be, which cannot exist, or which cannot act alone. It cannot live without God, nor can it eat, drink, love, or hate; it cannot justify itself or save itself; nor can it be sad or gay; nor can it hope or despair, succeed or fail. Thanks to God we exist among his creatures. Thus, truly, there are no human beings without God. There are some individuals who entertain this idea, who believe themselves atheists; it is an *idée fixe*. But that changes absolutely nothing; humanity as such is not without God. Human beings may behave as naughty children who cry and scold their mother. But their mother is there.

This is not a philosophical idea. I do not know whether one could explain, in a manner that might be convincing outside of faith in Jesus Christ, this affirmation: There is no humankind without God. But as soon as we have understood Jesus Christ, we have understood our humanity, our nature and our function, which are inseparable from God. Now, because there is no humankind without

God (atheism is a ridiculous invention), God commands us to pray, God participates in our affairs and in our needs, in our cares and in our distresses, in our expectations, in everything. When we pray, "Give us . . . our . . . bread," we do no other than to recognize what is the reality of our life; we admit that which is, namely, that we are nothing without him. And this command, this invitation to pray, to unite our cause with his, is a simple recognition of that which is: God invites and commands us to put ourselves beside Jesus Christ, who deigned to assume humanity. He was God, and he made himself a human being. Thus he interested himself in all these great things, and especially in all these small things, that preoccupy us.

The cause of the human race, that is, our material needs and our salvation, comes after God's. But notice that in it there is no question of optional requests. The first petitions would certainly not exist were it not for the last three, which are as indispensable as the others. If we would not continue to pray for the last three, we would not be praying with sincerity, for we too must have our place, since it is a question of our own cause, of all that we are, with our temperament, our nerves, and all the rest. We are not only there for God's cause; we must bring forward our own cause also, while making it fit into God's. It would therefore be dangerous to omit the last three petitions, for then there would be, on the one hand, an ecclesiastical, theological, metaphysical sphere, and, on the other hand, a sphere concerned with money, sex, business, and social relationships. There would thus be two compartments. Now, whether you wish it or not, there is only one. Nothing is so pernicious as the illusion of two compartments. You know how often ministers imagine that there are the two: this dialectic between God's cause and ours. However, they are linked together; we pray for the two as a whole. Such is the case because it is Jesus Christ who invites us to pray with him, because in him these two causes are one. Therefore it is important to understand in the Lord's Prayer the difference between these two parts, but also their unity.

Let us remember that in his Small Catechism Luther has emphasized this paradox in an interesting and enlightening manner: God acts in the direction that our prayer takes; he hallows his name, his kingdom comes, his will is done, he gives us our bread, he forgives us; he does all this before we pray. We address ourselves to him who has listened to us even before we say anything to him. Let us not forget this—and Luther was right when he said it—it is Jesus Christ who prays, and we join in his intercession. It is he whom God hears, and his prayer is heard since the beginning of the world, from eternity to eternity. Everything is already in order. In the first section of this work I have stressed, in accordance with Calvin and Luther, the foundations of prayer and God's response. Let us begin by understanding this: We are heard in the name of Jesus Christ. Everything is already there when we address ourselves to God.

As Luther says on the Lord's Prayer, we must take part in God's action. God is busy at work for his glory and for our salvation; and we ourselves must benefit from his action, not as spectators, nor by giving ourselves the role of indispensable collaborators, but by praying, by concerning ourselves with him, with what he is doing. Therein is the true collaboration. God invites us to address ourselves to him while understanding that his cause and ours are intimately united, that our cause is comprehended within his. We come, then, as human beings, and we are there before him, disposed to live in the wholeness of these two causes. All is contained in God's liberty, in his sovereignty. It is not a sort of necessity *(anagkē)*, of fatality; but God is our Father, and he wills that we be with him.

The First Three Petitions

"Hallowed be thy name."

When we speak of God, the name *(onoma)* signifies the glorious representation of God in the created world. Not simply and immediately identified with God himself, the name is the representation of God. Because the created world is the theater for God's glory (Calvin), the world is only a creature; it can become (but not in a philosophical sense), under certain conditions which do not depend upon itself, the bearer of God's name. There may happen to be in the world something like signs of God's name which indicate the presence of God himself. If such is the case, one may say that, like advertisements in our cities, these signs are not invisible, but they are illuminated by the revelation.

Our eyes are opened for us to see them. The world is God's world. This is why his name can be written upon it. The universe can sing his praise. Everything which is the creation of God can bear the name of its Creator.

Now let us ask the question: Is this name visible? Is it revealed? Are these signs illuminated? Are our eyes and ears opened? Is this name hallowed? We understand that this is an accomplishment not in the realm of possibility for the creature, which is of itself unable to become the bearer of God's name. The world as such has not the power to reveal God; and man as such is incapable of receiving a revelation, either by his eyes, his ears, or his understanding. It is God who knows how to speak of God

(Pascal).* In an act both objective and subjective, accomplished by himself, God causes himself to be seen, is seen, recognized, and appreciated, and we are permitted to live in this world in his presence, while knowing him, while recognizing him. This act of God becomes real for us in prayer.

The petition "Hallowed be thy name" implies that God's name is known to him who prays. One does not pray for something which one does not know. This presupposes that God's name is already hallowed (Luther). Thus, in the special situation of those who repeat the "Our Father" with Jesus Christ, we wish to obey the command to follow him also in prayer. And while we are praying with Jesus Christ, we are not ignorant of the hallowing of God's name in the past and in the present.

This prayer is then answered before we formulate it. We would not be Christians praying with Jesus Christ if our prayer meant that we know nothing of this hallowing. In fact, we pray in order that God's action, which is already taking place, may reach its end.

We must therefore transcribe these words, "Hallowed be thy name," in this way: "Thy name is already hallowed." Such a presupposition is the basis of prayer. Our Father, in heaven, thou hast spoken to us. In thy Son thou hast made thyself Word; thou hast made thyself perceptible and accessible to us in the flesh, in this world. The signs of thy name are not lacking illumination. We are not alone in this world. Thou hast taken a human face, which thou showest to us, and through it we can understand what thou sayest to us. We do not live in a world without God.

Thy prophets and thy apostles are on the same level as

*[Translator's Note] The original reads: *"C'est Dieu qui parle bien de Dieu."*

our life. We listen to them. Through thy church, the congregation of those whom thou hast called and whom thou
continuest to gather—thy church, which lives on the earth
and which has survived for so many centuries, in the midst
of so much upheaval, in terror and weakness—in spite of
all there is to be said of its faults, through it and its work
we have heard thy voice.

We are baptized, we exist in this church among thy
children, being ourselves thy children; we exist among
thy missionaries, among those whom thou hast charged
to announce thy word, and one cannot be a child of God
without being a missionary. We have the freedom to
believe, to will, and to obey. This means that the
world—this world in which we live—and our own life
with its limitations, its encumbrances, its difficulties, its
complications and those of our neighbor, cannot remain
for us an absolute mystery. There is much mystery, but
we do not live in an absolute mystery; we are not surrounded by nothingness. The doctrine of Sartre and
Heidegger is not true, for it sinks back into paganism.
We know that in this world, in this human state, in this
history, there is one thing certain: the signs of thy presence are luminous; Jesus Christ has died and risen for
us, and not only for us but for the whole world. Therefore, the hope of humanity rests upon this fact: God has
loved the world. Such is the reality shown by the death
and resurrection of the Lord. We live in the memory of
it and in the expectation of the general resurrection. It
is in this sense that we say, "God's name is already hallowed." This is the Christian position. The key of the
mystery is in our hands.

Let us go further. Because the key is given to us,
because God's name is already hallowed, we have all the
more reason to pray, "Hallowed be thy name." That

means: May it be given to us and to the world, to this world which is neither worse nor better than we are, in the midst of which we creatures have the advantage of knowing thee, of being called to thy service—may it be given to us to make use of thine incomparable offer; may it not be in vain that thou hast spoken to us in thy Son; may thy church know how to put its existence to work; may it be liberated from all Romanizing reaction and from all impetuous Americanism, from fear and faintheartedness, from the spirit of pride, from flippancy. May we stop leafing through the Bible instead of reading it. May we moderate a little our habit of quoting the Bible instead of living with it and letting it speak. May we pray that the Bible will not cease holding our attention. May the Bible not begin to make us yawn, and thy word, in all its parts, not become a boring matter in our minds and in our mouths; may it not become a bad sermon, a bad catechism, a bad theology. All these remarks are very simple, but also quite necessary.

Luther has explained at length that this hallowing must manifest itself in preaching. A bad sermon is the opposite of this hallowing. May God's word become anew for us each day the word of God. May it not be a truth, a principle, something which one places on the table, but a living person, the great mystery and the great simplicity. And may the signs of this word of God, of this name of God, be made visible through us, in the midst of us, by the severity and the serenity of our lives, of our customs, and of our ethics. We pray so that we may receive the power to show this great joy and this great peace of which we so often speak. May this joy and this peace be noticeable. We pray in order that the Christian arrogance and ignorance and unbelief with which we daily dishonor thee may be a bit arrested, a little suppressed.

May this key which has been put in our hands be turned ever so slightly so that the door can one day be opened. Herein is the hallowing of thy name. We see that there is reason to pray for these benefits and this fulfillment, so that what must still be done may be accomplished, although it cannot be done by us. In order that all this may be brought about, God himself must intervene; his cause is at stake. We who are responsible are so ill qualified to sustain this cause. How overwhelming it is for us to be responsible in this enterprise, and how absolutely necessary it is for God himself to intervene in order that we may not be among those foolish virgins who had no oil!

"Thy kingdom come."

We must go a little further than the Reformers, who have not discerned here or elsewhere the eschatological character of the reality of God's kingdom. We shall therefore give a slightly corrected version of their doctrine.

The kingdom of God in the New Testament is both the life and the purpose of the world according as they agree with the intentions of the Creator. It is the efficacious and definitive shield against the threat which followed and had to follow sin, against the fatal danger, the annihilation which lay in wait for the world because the world is only a creature. The kingdom of God is the final victory over sin. It is the reconciliation of the world to God (2 Cor. 5:19). And here is the consequence of this reconciliation: a new world, a new aeon, a new heaven, and a new earth, which are new because they are surrounded by the peace of God.

God's kingdom is the justice of God, the justice of the Creator, of the Lord, who justifies and triumphs. The end and purpose of the world is the coming of the kingdom:

"Thy kingdom come." It is clear that we are again confronted by an accomplishment which is infinitely beyond our possibilities, since all that we are, all that we can do, even under the most favorable conditions, is threatened by the same danger. We ourselves have need of this liberation, this victory, this reconciliation, this renewal. The coming of the kingdom is totally independent of our powers. We are as incapable of doing something toward its coming as creation itself, which is the replica of what we are and of what we are able to do. But it is for us an object of prayer. God alone, who has created the world, can complete it in this act of accomplishment, in this justification of himself and of his cross. It concerns the peace and the justice of a world which is brought to its perfection; and that can be only the result of his work. We must therefore pray, "Thy kingdom come!" Ring this bell to make known the hour of the event.

But saying to God "Thy kingdom come" presupposes that those who so pray know this kingdom, this life, this justice, this newness, this reconciliation; they know that all this is not foreign to them. They must know it, and when they pray in these words, the kingdom must already have come.

We find ourselves once more in this extraordinary situation of those who are praying the "Our Father" in the fellowship of Jesus Christ and of his own. "Thy kingdom come" is the same as saying, "Thy kingdom has already come; thou hast already established it in our midst." "The kingdom of God is in the midst of you" (Luke 17:21). Thou hast fulfilled all in Jesus Christ. Thou, God the Father, hast reconciled the world to thyself in Jesus Christ.

Paul does not speak of this reconciliation as of a future event. He says, "He reconciled." All this is done. In the person of Jesus Christ thou hast definitively destroyed sin and all its consequences. In him thou hast abolished all foreign and hostile powers: "I saw Satan fall like lightning from heaven" (Luke 10:18). Thou hast eliminated the fatal danger under the threat of which we were living. Thou, God, hast been in Jesus Christ the new man who will not die any more. All this is done. In him thy kingdom has been present in this world, in the depth, in the totality of his glory, without any attenuation or reticence. In Jesus Christ the world has reached its end and its purpose. Therefore, the last day, the judgment, the resurrection of the dead, all this is already fulfilled in him. It is not only an event to be awaited, it is behind us. We must understand that in him it is also a past event. When the church speaks of Jesus Christ, when it proclaims his word, when it believes in the gospel, when it goes out to the pagans to make known this gospel, when it prays to God, it looks backward to its Lord, who has already come. It remembers Christmas, Good Friday, Easter, and Pentecost. Those are not ordinary historical events to which we would give a mere religious significance (telling ourselves: that is all very well, but indeed that means nothing). No! They are not nothing. They are all that has happened and is behind us. We proclaim the word made flesh, and we announce the kingdom of God which has come. When it is not jubilant, when it is not sure of its significance, the church cannot be insistent and it is not insistent. A sad and gloomy church is not the church! For the church is built upon him who has been made flesh, upon him who has come to say the last word (not the next to the last). This last word has already been uttered. We live upon this event. There is nothing more in it to be changed. We cannot turn back time, whose beginning is Christmas and Easter.

What does this mean when we understand it, when we live it? This implies that we have the greater reason to pray, "Thy kingdom come!" Here is no contradiction. Those who believe these things to be true know it well. This is why they pray.

Furthermore, it means that this great movement of God in favor of the human race which began with Christmas, with Easter, and with Pentecost must be recaptured, in order that it not be merely an event behind us, because we live not only by looking backward, but also by looking ahead. It must come, the future must bear the marks of the past, our past must become our future, and the Lord who has come must come again.

We pray for the removal of this covering which now conceals all things, as the cloth which covers this table [here Barth indicates a table covered by a cloth]. The table is underneath [he raps on the table]. You hear it. But you do not see it. You have only to remove the cloth to see it. We pray in order that the covering which still veils the reality of the kingdom may be removed, in order that the reality of everything already changed in Jesus Christ may be made visible. All of God's depth is there. This is the fact beside which nothing else can be measured. Our personal life and that of our family, the life of the churches, the political events, all these are the covering. The reality is beneath it. We do not yet see face to face; we see, as in a mirror, indistinct reflections. We cannot be sure of our position when we read the newspapers, religious or otherwise. For us to see the reality, thy kingdom must come, Jesus Christ must become visible, even as he was visible at Easter, even as he revealed himself to his apostles. He will be, he is already now, the head of the new humankind in the new world. We know this, but we do not yet see it. We wait to see it; we walk by faith, not yet by sight.

May the light of God which was in Jesus Christ, in his life, in his death and resurrection, be shed over us, over our whole life, and over all things. May the secret of earthly life be revealed. This secret has already been revealed, but we do not yet see it. Hence this anxiety in which we live, these cares, these exaggerations, these despairs. We do not understand. And we pray that we may be granted the power to see and to understand.

Now let us return to the exegesis of the Reformers. When we pray, may we also receive the power to see, right now, at least the first signs of this new age, of this victory which has already been won. May the dawn of this universal day enable us to see ourselves and others as well as the events of our history, in the light of that which is coming ahead of us. This general revelation, this *apoka-lypsis* (1 Peter 1:3–12) will be given to us. May our faith in him who has come be made alive. It cannot be so unless it is founded on the event of the past, and unless it looks toward what is coming, toward that which will reveal the universality of his work. May we receive the gift of living that hope. One cannot say, "Thy kingdom come!" without hope for our time, for today, for tomorrow. The great Future, with a capital F, is also a future with a small *f*. That is enough to make us understand, at least in a small way, the total insufficiency of all our works in the present, the pettiness of all the conflicts in which we struggle, especially in our personal, psychological conflicts, which basically cannot be justified. But in order to understand this, we must see the kingdom which is to come. The psychologists cannot help us. Someday the sun will rise, knowledge will be given us. We are waiting only until Easter becomes for the world a general event. We shall then no longer have need of psychologists, because there will be health. It is amazing to note how we Swiss—with even more naïveté than the other modern Europeans—are interested in psychology, whereas in Germany, for instance, all these conflicts have disappeared because of the immediacy of life with all its exigencies. When life is there, we have no more psychological problems.

We pray in order that we may receive the gift of seeing the uselessness of this tragic sense which befits the pagans, not the Christians. May we live at once in tranquillity, in good humor, and in the love that constrains on one but may in some way attract people.

A variant reading of the Lord's Prayer in Luke's text adds, "Thy Holy Spirit come upon us and purify us." It is an interesting variant, although only the traditional texts of Matthew and Luke are authentic. Nevertheless, this is a commentary well adapted to the text. If one prays for the coming of God's kingdom, one prays also that the Holy Spirit may come within us. The Reformers explained the second petition as if they had taken this variant into account. Indeed they were right, but this cannot be done unless the words "thy kingdom" are understood to mean something quite different from a perfect church; unless they are understood as the end of that which is now and as the advent of a new state of things. Fortunately, in the kingdom of God there will no longer be need of the church, for Jesus Christ will have finished what he has begun.

We must still pray to God, for it is his cause that matters. His commandments are a constant reminder of his patience with us. During the disquieting time of the exercise of his patience, while we are still separated from the coming of his kingdom, how necessary it is for God to have his say, for him to make this bell ring! Yes, this time must come to an end! May God fulfill his promises, and may we lay hold of them as promises of God. "Thy kingdom come"—this kingdom that has already come. Such is our prayer, simple, quite close to him, habitual.

"Thy will be done on earth as it is in heaven."

We return to the present, which, like the past, belongs also to the realm of God's will, the realm in which is carried out the plan he has made to legitimize himself, to glorify himself as Creator and as Lord, and at the same time to justify and glorify his creature. This creature, in comparison to him, is small, weak, and threatened by many dangers, prone to failure because it is contaminated by sin, lost, reduced to nought. But the will of God is to maintain his creature, to save it, and to fulfill his work by the manifestation of his kingdom.

"Thy will . . ." Let the plan be executed, let its consummation come to pass now, between the beginning and the end. May this time we are living out not be in vain. The fulfillment cannot be our own. It is not we who do this will of God. To him belong the plan and its execution, to him belongs the time, both the present and the future—all the categories of time. Thus we find ourselves faced with a third object of prayer: may God deign to trouble himself with us and with this world; may he not tire, not cease being patient; may he continue to reign until the end. Yet while praying thus, we must know that this is taking place, that God is engaged in carrying out his will, in accomplishing it. We pray the "Our Father" in communion with Jesus Christ, and we know consequently that his will is already done.

"As . . . in heaven . . ." I hope I do not misinterpret these words. Thy will is already done, according to thy intentions, eternal God. It has been done, it will be done, and it will further unfold itself in time. But before now this will has been done in him, in the mystery of what has taken place and of what is taking place with him. It has been done in his creation, in his governing of the world since the beginning; in the history of his covenant, which faithfully expresses the meaning of all events—the covenant such as it was understood by the prophets and the apostles and whose testimony was given us in Jesus Christ. It is thy will even as thou knowest it, even as thy angels see it, even as it is "at thy right hand"; even as we believe it (although we do not see it). It is done and it is being done ceaselessly in heaven.

It is being done as it must be done, in the full knowledge of the case; it is being done without let or hindrance, in complete freedom, in such a manner that grace alone prevails and thankfulness on the part of the creature makes answer to it. It is so done in Jesus Christ. In heaven it is perfectly fulfilled. And on account of Jesus Christ we know it. His Spirit teaches and confirms it to us. His will is done and is always being done.

We have therefore the more reason to pray that his will be done "on earth" as it is in heaven. May its execution be realized in our world and in our lives, according to what we know of it, according to what it appears to be with the covering. May the fulfillment of his will become consonant on earth with its fulfillment in heaven: *Sicut in caelo, et in terra.* This means: may the *chiaroscuro*, this mixture of our secular and ecclesiastical history, this mixture of sanctity and stupidity, of wisdom and vulgarity, which characterizes much of our existence—may all this confusion be dispelled. In heaven his will is perfectly done. Why not among us? May this *chiaroscuro* not last forever; may we cease misunderstanding, thwarting thy intentions. May we cease contradicting and falsifying thy gospel again and again, in an attempt to make of it a new kind of law. May we renounce behaving like bad servants. May we employ thy patience for our conversion instead of toying with a humanistic Christianity and a Christian humanism, instead of continually provoking thy wrath. In the execution of thy plan, liberate us from this endless imperfection of our obedience. Come to give us freedom and, someday, extricate us from these contradictions in which we find ourselves—we who know that thy will is done and how it is done in heaven.

Once more it is God's cause that is in question. And we participate in his cause even as he participates in ours. His cause cannot be foreign to us. We are in the present, within time. Now, this time is very short; life passes very quickly. There is not a moment to lose—and we lose so many! What can be expected of the world if we Christians are so abstractedly earthly, so complacent in our imperfection, so much at ease when it should not be possible for us to be? God reigns. We pray that he may let us reign with him. No less than that.

The Last Three Petitions

First let us note the change of attitude in the second part of the Lord's Prayer, which begins with the request, "Give us." In the first three petitions our prayer is a sort of conversation with the heavenly Father. It is like a sigh. We are dazzled by the grandeur of what occupies us: the name, the kingdom, the will of God himself. We sigh and pray from a certain distance, in a manner almost indirect, "Thy name . . . thy kingdom . . . thy will." With the last three petitions we come to prayer properly speaking. Nevertheless, as we shall notice, this real change is in keeping with the first three petitions.

Here we shall make two remarks:

1. The *"us"* of the Lord's Prayer now becomes explicit and audible. Eight times in these three verses we find the words "our," "we," or "us." We recall that the "us" of the "Our Father" is, so to speak, created by the invitation, the command of Jesus Christ, "Follow me." The "us" means those who wish to learn to pray with Jesus Christ.

Apropos of this "us," let us note four points:

a. The "us" refers to the fellowship of those who are with Jesus Christ, the God-Man, who permits and commands them to join him, to join in his own intervention with God, to pray with him.

b. It is the "us" of the fellowship which unites people together at the same time as they are united with Jesus Christ, united together by this permission and this command. It is, however, not a closed fellowship; it is open in the sense that it is involved in this world, that it represents the world, if "world" is understood to mean all those who have not yet heard and followed the Lord's invitation.

c. The "us" of these last three petitions concerns the unified community, which thinks and acts in solidarity; which knows, through a deep experience, the misery of the human condition. However, in the midst of this distress, of which it is aware, the community is free to address itself to God in communion with Jesus Christ, who is raised from the dead, and in common accord with those who make up his community; it is free to address itself to our Father who is in heaven, to the sovereign Creator, Lord, and Savior, in order to obtain from him a complete and final deliverance, knowing that this Sovereign can and will grant it.

d. It is the "us" of those who—because they are united with Jesus Christ crucified and because they have the freedom to pray with him as members of God's family—on account of this fact alone know what is their own misery and the misery of the world, the profound malignity and the incurable sadness of human existence, the fall and perdition of God's good creature. They know the inability of human beings to extricate themselves from this situation by their own resolves, by their own efforts; they know the unconditional necessity of submitting themselves to God, of trusting God alone; in short, they grasp the impossibility of living otherwise than in free grace. Observe that "us" means those who implicitly, in an inaudible way, have already prayed the first three petitions, which were concerned with the glory and the cause of God himself. In these last three petitions, it is the same people ("us") who come forward with their own cause.

2. A second remark: In these three petitions, prayer now becomes explicit, direct, and imperative. It is one thing to pray, "Thy name . . . thy kingdom . . . thy will," and another thing to say, "Give us this day . . . forgive us . . . lead us not . . . deliver us." Notice the boldness, I shall even say the temerity, of this appeal. Here is the person who dares to importune God, asking him to concern himself with human affairs; here is the person who dares such imperative language. How can this be done? We reply: We are the only ones to whom it is permitted, nay, even commanded, in the first three petitions, to concern ourselves with God's affairs, with the hallowing of his name, with the coming of his kingdom, with the doing of his will. Is this our concern? Yes, certainly. We are permitted to attend to it. God has accepted us as co-workers (this is a biblical expression). He has made his cause our own. And now, as a consequence of these first three petitions, our appeal to God becomes, so to speak, quite natural in the three that follow. We say: "Our Father, here we are just as thou findest us, exactly as we are, and, it well seems, in the

state in which thou desirest to meet us. Here we are, engrossed in thy cause (we presume that our prayer is earnest), kindled by the ardent desire to see thy name hallowed. We have no other task; this is our care. It is not a question of our being able to help ourselves. Any preoccupation of this kind could only be infidelity, disloyalty, disobedience. Therefore, to thee we hand over our existence—to thee, who hast invited and commanded us to pray, to live for thy cause. Here we are. It is now up to thee to concern thyself with our human cause."

From this springs the audacity of these three petitions. They express such an action on our part. When we ask God to give us all we need, both outwardly and inwardly, for our existence, we comply with his command to serve him for the sake of his glory.

In the first three petitions, Jesus Christ asks us to join with him in his fight for God's cause, and at the same time he invites us to share in his victory over the world, over everything that could hinder the realization of the sighs that are uttered in these petitions. Jesus Christ has vanquished, and he invites us now to participate in his victory. In order that we may have the freedom to utter these sighs, "Thy name . . . thy kingdom . . . thy will," we avail ourselves of the invitation that Jesus Christ extends to us for the partaking of his victory. Herein lies the good and true reason for what I have called the boldness, the temerity, of this appeal: "Give us . . . forgive us"; this is the reason for our daring to accost God in this manner. For this appeal is astonishing, let us admit. It cannot be made except in the liberty that issues from the pledge we make as children of God, brothers and sisters in Jesus Christ.

These are the two essential aspects of what I call the change of attitude between the two parts of the Lord's Prayer. This change is, after all, only the consequence of the freedom that dominates the first part of the Lord's Prayer.

Let us now proceed to the interpretation. We must not forget, however, that any development can be only tentative. We shall follow the same order as previously: first, the explanation of terms; then, the way in which God hears and has already heard this prayer; and finally, an examination of the prayer itself.

We must recall that the Reformers, Luther and Calvin, never ceased emphasizing this point: God has already heard our prayer, and on account of this fact we have the freedom and we receive the command to pray. No petition of the Lord's Prayer can be understood in any other way.

"[Give us this day] our daily bread."

By the words "our . . . bread," some of the Reformers have included (and we can do so with them) all that we need for existence.

Those who are acquainted with Luther's Small Catechism will remember the famous list that he draws up to explain the meaning of the word "bread": food, drink, clothes, shoes, houses, farms, fields, lands, money, property, a good marriage, good children, honest and faithful public servants, a just government, favorable weather (neither too hot nor too cold!), health, honors, good friends, loyal neighbors. That is no small order! This list contains the necessities and requirements for the life of a German "bourgeois" farmer in the sixteenth century. And nothing hinders us from interpreting and expanding it according to the needs of our time and of our individual situations. We are certainly permitted to think of our daily bread in the wide sense of the term. Nevertheless, I wish to emphasize that it is advisable for us not to lose sight of the original word "bread" in all its simplicity. In the biblical language "bread" has two meanings:

1. It is the strict necessity for life, the minimum nourishment which the poor cannot do without; it is the necessary minimum for the beggar, for the tramp. It is opposed to the idea of hunger. Asking God to give us bread means having recourse to his free grace, which upholds and maintains us at the brink of the abyss of hunger and death. This minimum allows us to live today. Shall we have it tomorrow also? This is the vital question. Now we live on it. But tomorrow? No one knows. There is no guarantee that God will give us this necessary bread and, with our bread, life. The children of God know this precariousness of our existence and of the human situation in general. Whether rich or poor, they know that we are a people in the wilderness; we are this people of Israel preoccupied with the cause of God. This is why we dare to ask him to save us from hunger and death. We ask it in this utterly primitive form, "bread," because we should not take it for granted that we shall have it tomorrow.

2. In the Old and New Testaments the word "bread" is also the temporal sign of God's eternal grace. The word contains a meaning far more simple, natural, and material, and at the same time far more profound and sublime, than we suppose. These qualities of the natural and the sublime are intimately linked. They are a sign from God, given to this people in the wilderness, given to the poor, the afflicted, those who are hungry and thirsty, those who are in the jaws of death. On account of this, bread is something sacred. Bread is the promise, and not only the promise but also the mysterious presence, of this food which nourishes once and for all. Bread is the mysterious

presence of this food which, after it has been eaten, does not need to be replaced. In the Bible each meal, whether it be modest or sumptuous, is something sacred, for it is the promise of an eternal banquet, of an everlasting feast. In the Bible bodily and temporal life is sacred because it is the promise of the life immortal and eternal.

This word "bread," as we have seen, is put in juxtaposition with the word "hunger." But it is also associated with that fullness of life which we shall know in the new era, in the world to come. This real bread which we eat is the pledge and also the sign—and at the same time as it is the sign, it is the presence—of this fullness. This is what is called here "our bread." "Give us . . . our . . . bread" means then: "Give us this minimum which is necessary for the present moment; and at the same time, give it to us as a sign, as a pledge anticipating our whole life. According to thy promise, which we are receiving at this moment, we receive also the presence of thine eternal goodness, the assurance that we shall live with thee."

Considerable discussion has been raised on the subject of the adjective "daily." This word presents all sorts of enigmas; these problems I shall not bring up here. I shall merely suggest to you the most probable answer. *Epiousios* (daily) means, "For each day, for the coming day." Give us today our bread for each day, the bread that we shall need tomorrow. We live in the present, but shall we be alive at the next minute, the next day? Until then will hunger and thirst spare us? This is the concrete question which confronts us with the precariousness of our condition. You will recall that in Matthew 6, Jesus exhorts us not to be anxious about our life, what we shall eat or what we shall drink. Calvin was certainly correct when he added, in his commentary, "We must work well in order to assure our food of the morrow."

However, neither anxiety nor work provides an answer to this question, Shall we be alive tomorrow? Prayer must take the place of anxiety and form the basis of work for the morrow. The children of God are not anxious about work. They work because they pray.

But is it not at this point that the other meaning of the word "bread" must intervene? Anxiety for the temporal morrow prefigures anxiety for the eternal morrow. For this temporal precariousness cannot be compared to the precariousness of human destiny. "What then shall I say, poor man that I am?" as it is written in the requiem. May this fear be transformed and may it become a prayer. The children of God, who know the uncertainty of human life and all that is for us an object of fear in time and in eternity, hope to receive today, yes, today, with their bread and in the form of earthly bread, the pledge, even the first-fruits, of the bread that will feed them eternally, that will feed them on this eschatological morrow.

Let us now look into the meaning of the whole sentence. Praying God to give us our bread both earthly and celestial, both substantial and supersubstantial, presupposes that we know God as the giver. We have already said that in order to pray with full knowledge of the case, we must pray with the certainty of a reply. Praying at random, without this certainty, is not praying. Therefore, our prayer must begin with this implication: Thou givest us our bread for tomorrow, yes, thou givest it us today. Thou art our faithful Creator, and thou dost not cease being so for an instant. We are a people in the wilderness, and yet we find ourselves surrounded by the splendors and the riches of creation, and by all the creatures, and by this covenant of grace which thou hast desired to establish between thyself and us. Thou desirest not our death, but our life.

On thy side, in what concerns thee, absolutely nothing can be lacking. There is abundant bread for us and for all those who might unite with us in this prayer; there is abundant bread for everyone. No risk other than hunger and death can surprise us. Thou art ready to maintain all whom thou hast willed to call for the service of thy glory. Everything thou givest us is truly the pledge of a living food, of this fullness in which we shall live eternally. This we know because thou art our Father in heaven, our Father in Jesus Christ, with whom we live. He has called us to follow him. We accompany him, for the moment from afar—nevertheless, we accompany him. And since thou art his Father, thou art also ours; on this account we know that thou hast prepared for us the meal, the complete feast, both temporal and eternal. We listen to thy voice, which invites us to be the guests of thy table. We need to hear this voice which summons us, and we cannot forget it: "Come; for all is now ready." This is what impels us to pray and gives us the freedom to say to God, "Give us this day our daily bread."

We must also say: "Act in such a way that thou dost not give it us in vain, so that we may truly receive this bread which thou hast prepared on thy table in the holy Communion, so that we may take from thy hands this bread which thou hast created for us and which thou givest us. Help us, then; illumine us. May we not behave like well-satisfied bourgeois or like greedy creatures at the moment when thou bestowest upon us anew this incomprehensible and incomparable gift, this gift of thy patience, and of our hope. Act in such a way that we do not squander and destroy this gift. Grant that we may each receive our bread without dispute or quarrel. Grant that all who have a surplus of this bread may know by this very fact that they are appointed as servants, as dispensers of thy grace, that they are in thy service and in the service of others. And grant that those who are particularly threatened by hunger, death, and this precariousness of the human condition may meet brothers and sisters who have open eyes and ears and feel their responsibility. How shameful is our social ingratitude and injustice! How senseless it is that in this humanity surrounded by thy gifts there are people still dying of hunger!

"Act in such a way that we may receive the food essential to us, that we may receive it as thou givest it to us, that is, as a sign and a promise. And while we are using the fruits of this sign, while we are blessing thee ('Bless the Lord, O my soul, and forget not all his benefits'), may we enjoy beforehand the presence of the things that thou dost promise to us, and already today may we participate in this feast which thou wilt preside over from everlasting to everlasting."

As you see, there is reason to pray! Yes, it is our cause that is at stake. We are entirely dependent upon God. He really must make our cause his own, so that it may be upheld and victorious. And we are there, we, who are free to invoke him fearlessly, with the certainty that he listens. For whatever we ask of him he has always done and will always do.

"Forgive us our offenses [debts].*"*

What we translate in French as *nos offenses* means literally, "our faults," that is to say, it suggests that we are in default in our relation to God, in what we owe him. We have a debt due to him, and if we cannot pay it, we remain in default. If one does not fulfill an incumbent obligation, one is in default. One may be righteous, nevertheless one is guilty. The result is that we offend the one with whom we are at fault.

We are God's debtors. We owe him not something, whether it be little or much, but, quite simply, our person in its totality; we owe him ourselves, since we are his creatures, sustained and nourished by his goodness. We, his children, called by his word, admitted to the service of his glorification—we, brothers and sisters of the man Jesus Christ—come short of what we owe to God. What we are and what we do correspond in no wise to what is given us. We are his children and we know not how to recognize it. Calvin says, "Whoever refuses to confess that we offend God, as debtors who do not pay, excludes himself from Christianity." And Luther, "Before God everyone is compelled to lower his plumes." Thus, in Christianity we acknowledge this state of things, and we find ourselves incapable of setting it right. While we avail ourselves of his invitation and try to obey in doing these things, we who pray mingle in them our own ideas, our own inclinations, our ethics, our religion, and we find ourselves obliged to admit ever anew that we are unworthy to serve him. When we look at ourselves, we know we are without hope before him.

For even when we live as Christians, we increase our debt, we aggravate the "mess" of our situation. It grows from day to day. And I think that the older one becomes, the more one realizes that there is no hope for us. Matters go from bad to worse. We find ourselves rejected at the very beginning of the Lord's Prayer and confronted by this question: How can we have the audacity to draw near to God? In showing our zeal for his cause and then in flaunting before him our own needs, who are we to have the pretense of being co-workers with God? And who are we to say to God, "Take care of me, of us! Give us!" We who are his debtors! Once again everything seems to be called into question.

What does the word "forgive" mean? In the pure, ideal sense, it signifies, "Regard our debtor as though he or she had done us no wrong." It means not imputing to such persons their fault, not holding rigorously against them this guilt in which they find themselves, in which they see themselves. On the contrary, let us turn over a new leaf with such persons, giving them another chance. "Forgive us!" This request excludes any sort of pretense on our part. It debars us from the right, no matter how small, of making any claim whatever with God. Neither human debt nor human beings themselves as debtors can be pardoned. The human race is insolvent, and has no right to claim remission of its debt. The right of placing the guilty again in the position of children of God can belong only to him whom we have offended; this can be only the right of the creditor or of the sovereign whom we have deceived, in whose service we have defaulted and we still default. This right can belong only to the free mercy of God. We ask of God, then, that he be willing to use this right which is in his grace. We can have confidence in him. But without totally renouncing all rights whatever on our part, we would not know how to pray as we ought.

> *"As we also forgive those who have offended us*
> [As we also have forgiven our debtors]."

Does this sentence imply a kind of previous condition which we should set for ourselves in order to obtain God's forgiveness? No, it is a criterion necessary for our understanding of God's pardon. For those who know that they are cast upon the mercy of God, that they cannot exist without the divine forgiveness—those who have lived such an experience—cannot do otherwise than to forgive their fellow human beings, those who have offended against them (we are all offenders, debtors one to another, and we are so daily). Even if the debts of our offenders appear to us to be very heavy, they are always infinitely lighter than ours with God. How could we, who ourselves are such great debtors, hope to have the divine forgiveness if we did not of ourselves wish to do this small thing, namely, to forgive those who have offended us? The hope one entertains for oneself necessarily opens the heart, the feeling, and the judgment, in respect to others. To know how to forgive is not a merit, a moral effort, or a sort of virtue. How irritating are those people who, with a perpetual smile, run after you to forgive you!

Human forgiveness is a beautiful thing, an almost physical necessity. In the light of the divine forgiveness, we see those poor creatures who have offended us, and even in difficult cases we think that, after all, the matter is not so serious. Let us not settle down to enjoy the offenses done to us; let us not nurse our grudges with pleasure. Rather, let us retain some humor with respect to our offenders. Let us have toward others this small impulse of forgiveness, of freedom. This act must not be looked upon as a piece of moral armor belonging to a good Christian knight. It is neither a helmet nor a saber which could make us bold and strong, but something that must be natural. Those who do not have this very small freedom are not within reach of divine forgiveness. It might be said of such persons that they do not know how to pray, that they cannot then receive anything. Thus, we are not faced with an exhortation, "Go, forgive," but we are confronted by a simple recognition of a fact: When the pardon of God is received, it enables us to forgive. The pardon of God is something that occurs at the divine level. One cannot draw a comparison with what happens at the human level; nevertheless, on that plane this little matter of forgiving offenses must come to pass. How shall I hope for something for myself if I do not even grant it to my neighbor?

I cannot escape the obligation of giving this small token! And by so doing I shall not make myself worthy to receive God's forgiveness. I shall simply validate my hope and my prayer.

What God's forgiveness is must be clearly understood. Here it is not a question of an uncertain hope, of an ideal to be sought or imagined. It is a fact. Even before I ask it, God has already granted his pardon. He who does not know that prays in vain. Forgiveness is already given, and this is the reality by which we live.

"Our Father who art in heaven . . ." Yes, thou hast forgiven us our offenses. Before I say to thee, "Forgive me," thou hast established and announced thy right of pardon, the justice of thy mercy, thy right of overlooking our faults and of not regarding us as offenders. In thy Son thou hast exchanged the roles between thyself, the holy and just God, and us, perfidious and unjust human beings. Thou hast put thyself in our place so as to reestablish order in our favor. Thou hast obeyed and suffered for us; thou hast abolished our faults, the faults of all humankind. And thou hast done it once and for all.

Thou hast annulled our faults, which accompany us from the moment of our birth until our death, and also those we commit each day, at every instant, in one manner or another. Thou hast annulled those faults that we know only too well and also the others that we do not know how to see and that will be revealed one day when the account book is presented. Then we shall see ourselves as we are in thy sight. Thou hast abolished all these faults; thou hast begotten a new creature (a new "us" and a new "me") without faults, without offenses—a person well-pleasing to thee, who is upright in thy eyes, pure and spotless, without reproach. Thou hast begotten this human being and thou hast brought us together around him, around the cross of thy Son, in order that we may be witnesses at our own judgment, because we must indeed take part in this judgment, in this death which he endured in our place, for our liberation.

Thou hast given us thy Holy Spirit in order that the work of this creation which thou hast accomplished in this new human being, Jesus Christ, may become a living thing in us; in order that thy grace, displayed in this event, may become ours. Because thou hast done all this in thy Son, and because thou hast acted by thy Holy Spirit, thou allowest us no longer to doubt, to remain in uncertainty and uneasiness, in the presence of our offenses. Henceforth our faults are thy concern, not ours. Thou forbiddest us to look backward, to feel ourselves overwhelmed as though chained to our past, to what we are and do today, and even to what we shall be and do tomorrow.

This habit of always casting our eyes on our own sin, instead of looking up to thee, is gone. Thou hast severed us from this past. In Jesus Christ thou hast made me a new creature. Thou permittest and commandest me to look ahead. We shall not live by taking lightly what we are or do, or what we have been and have done; nor shall we live by putting all our trust in what we shall be and do. On the contrary, we shall live by being always on guard, in the knowledge that we are and always shall be judged, and also by putting our trust in thee and in what thou hast done, in this judgment that thou hast pronounced, in this death that thou hast suffered for us. It is a question of something already fulfilled *(tetelesthai)*. However, this perfect tense is also for us a future tense which thou hast procured for us. We have only to walk on this road which lies open in the direction of our future. By forgiving us thou hast given us the freedom to travel on it.

Nevertheless, we must thoroughly understand that it is not possible for us to speak seriously in this fashion with God, nor to receive his pardon, unless we pray, "Forgive us our offenses." It is now a matter of tending toward this perfect future. It is up to us to believe, to realize this beginning which was inaugurated by the death of Jesus Christ.

May we, therefore, live our life such as it is, that is to say, united with his; may we take our place where he has placed us, where we are in reality, where he has suffered, obeyed, and lived for us. May we put on this new humanity which God has begotten in Christ. May we not live in just any way, but in the reality of what God has done for us. May we not vex the Holy Spirit when he assures us that we are thy children and that we are thine not by our own merits but on account of thy free mercy, because thou hast vanquished sin in the flesh and exalted thy poor creature to the heights of heaven. May thy forgiveness sanctify us ever increasingly in spite of all that we have been, in spite of what we still are and shall be. We know that our sanctity will never be other than thine and that it will triumph out of our distress, out of all our impurities. Yes, may thy forgiveness sanctify us until that day when, with the return of thy Son, thou wilt reveal to us for the last time, displayed in thy light, all wherein we have failed, our turpitude, our faults, all that we have hidden. But, more important still, thou wilt reveal to us thy right to forgive us, the justice of thy mercy, which has prevailed over our misery. "Forgive us": give us today, and all the days which thy patience still grants us, to live in the freedom of this forgiveness which thou hast bestowed upon us.

in thy design, which is always good." We are wrong when we cry, "Deliver us from any possible danger or cause for sorrow." In the sixth petition of the Lord's Prayer we are not concerned with evils of this sort, with these minor temptations, which are of a relative and bearable nature.

There is, nevertheless, the great temptation, the eschatological temptation, which may, of course, be manifested in a minor temptation, but which is intrinsically something else; it is the work of the Evil One. Moral and physical trials may, in fact, be identified with it; they may be the expression of its deadly action. However, one must distinguish between the two, for here it is not a matter of an ordinary threat which might be clearly perceived and resisted. It is rather a question of the infinite menace of the nothingness that is opposed to God himself. It is the menace that, for the creature, carries with it not only a passing danger, a destruction of secondary importance, a momentary corruption, but total fall, ultimate extinction. This is the supreme temptation. In it there is nothing good, nothing that can be of any use to us. It is without fruits, and if it reaches us, one cannot say of it, "Rejoice." It is without hope. There is an intolerable, unendurable evil that in no way competes with the good. This threat exists; it manifests its presence. This supreme and infinite evil does not belong to creation. There are some evils pertaining to creation; as we have said, they are relative and bearable. But this one is not part of that which God has willed and created. It is at the limits of his creation, on the left side, even as God himself is on the limits of it on the right. This absolute evil imposes itself upon creation in the form that we all recognize, namely, sin and death. It appears in the illegitimate dominion, incomprehensible and inexplicable, of the one whom the Scriptures call the Devil. The creature is defenseless in the face of this threat.

God is superior to it, but not the creature. Once given entrance, the Devil performs endless ravages against which we have no other protection than God's. Wherever God is absent, wherever he is not the master, it is the other one who dominates. There is no alternative.

Our Reformers, Luther as well as Calvin, were acquainted not only with the small temptations but also with the great one. They knew it was with the Devil that they had to deal. For him they had no respect, since he is not respectable. But they knew that he exists. They did not reckon only with the malice of men, the pope and all those who opposed their action. No, they knew that there is not merely the opposition of men. There is the Evil One, who makes evil everything that preoccupies us and causes us anxiety. God's enemy is also the enemy of God's creature. In order for us rightly to pray this last petition, we must know that the Reformers held the correct view.

Far from me be the idea of preaching the Devil to you. One cannot preach him, and I do not at all intend to cause you anguish. Nevertheless, there is in this matter a reality that we modern Christians pass over too lightly. There exists a superior, ineluctable enemy whom we cannot resist unless God comes to our aid. I do not care for demonology, nor for the manner in which it is treated in Germany today and perhaps elsewhere. Ask me no questions about the Demon, for I am not an authority on the subject! However, it is necessary for us to know that the Devil exists, but then we must hasten to get away from him.

We pray thee, our Father, to lead us in such a way that it may be given us to avoid this limit on the left, this pernicious boundary. Lead us, for we are thy children, saved through Jesus Christ. Spare us not from struggle (which we must accept), not from sufferings (which we must endure), but spare us from the encounter with this enemy, who is stronger than all our strength, more clever than our intelligence (including the intelligence we put into our theology), more dangerously sentimental—for the Devil is also sentimental—than we ourselves are capable of being. He is more pious (yes, the Devil is pious too) than all our Christian piety, both ancient and modern, or theological. Shield us from all possibility of evil from which we know not how to preserve ourselves, since it would utterly and irrevocably degrade us to the level of brutes.

For us this is not one temptation among many others, not one a shade more sad and somber, but it is the supreme temptation, whereby the impossible becomes possible.

"Deliver us from the Evil One." We perceive and feel his power. To tell the truth, it is only a pseudo power. It is not a real power. The terrible thing about it is that it acts, although this action is unreal. It is useless to minimize it even though it is unreal. The danger lies in the fact that it is a sly, insidious power. Yet it reigns in a sense that is only too real. It has power over us because we are sinners. We have yielded to it. We are in the jaws of death. We complain of it, we suffer from it, but we cannot break loose.

The Greek word means not only "deliver us" but "snatch us from these jaws." In the Old Testament the psalms resound from beginning to end with the cry "Snatch us." And Christianity takes up this cry in the sixth petition. For it is acquainted with this enemy, because it knows Jesus Christ. It knows that he has faced not only the ill will of the human race but also the enemy of God and of his creature. There had to be the Son of God to unmask the sinister wickedness of the enemy. That is why the Lord's Prayer ends with this *de profundis*. If our prayer is not terminated by this *de profundis*, it does not answer what Jesus Christ has taught us.

However, this final petition also presupposes what we well know about this danger on the left: God has already done what we ask him. He has done it before we have even thought of praying thus, before we have formulated this petition: "Lead us not into temptation." Now, God does not drive us into this temptation. No, our Father, thou dost not do it. How couldst thou do it, thou who hast revealed thyself in thy Son? Thou art not double-faced. Thy attitude toward the great temptation is not equivocal; it is categorical. Thy resistance to it is clear and forthright. Thus it has been since the first day of creation, ever since thou hast said, "Let there be light!" Thou, our Father, hast no acquaintance with evil, thou knowest no compromise with it, thou dost not tolerate it. The threat of nothingness will never be a threat coming from thee; it will never be tolerated or admitted by thee. On the contrary, by directing us in thy paths, in the paths of thy gifts, of thy pardon, thou wilt never lead us to the left, but always to the right. We can be sure that when we follow thy word, we shall not be led into the great temptation. By following the path which thou hast prepared for us and which thou hast revealed in thy Son, we shall always be shielded from this aberration. Thou wilt deliver us from the Evil One.

Art thou not God the Liberator? One alone is able to liberate us in a decisive manner. It is thou. We know now that thou art the great liberator. Thou hast personally opposed thyself to the Evil One, to this usurper whose sway must be abolished because it has nothing to do with thy creation. Thou hast stepped forward to break the powers of this realm of the Devil. Thou hast caused the Devil to fall like lightning from the sky; we have seen him fall. Thou hast triumphed over the shadows by the resurrection of thy Son. Thou hast proclaimed thy victory by many signs and miracles; and thou proclaimest it still among us by baptism in the name of thy Son and by the presence of his body and his blood in the Holy Supper.

Thou hast already snatched us from those jaws. Thine be the glory! We no longer have to let ourselves be affected by the threat of the Evil One, nor do we need to fear it. And this is why we pray, "Lead us not into temptation, but deliver us from the Evil One." Be present in our midst, thou faithful and infallible guide, thou who showest us thy way and openest it before our feet. Thou art the victorious leader, before whom the Evil One is but an idiot, a ridiculous scarecrow, a nonentity.

We know that without thee this would not be so. Our paths would not be the right path. Our moral and religious excursions could never succeed. Without thee our undertakings in the conquest of temptation, evil, and the Devil would only aggravate the situation. To thee alone belongs the right to protect us, to snatch us from this position. Once again: Glory be to thee, in whom we put our trust! That is the ultimate freedom which God grants us.

There is reason to pray. Without this final petition in the Lord's Prayer and without the answer which precedes our prayer, we would be not only disabled and judged but also reduced to nothingness. Thine be the glory! Thou hast annihilated him who wished to annihilate us. Thou hast loved us; thou still lovest us. And thy love is efficacious. It delivers once and for all.

The Doxology

"For thine is the kingdom and the power and the glory, forever."

Of this we shall speak briefly.

These words do not belong to the original text of the Gospel. They are not authentic; there is no doubt about this. They constitute an adjunction, an enlargement, introduced for the liturgical usage of the Lord's Prayer. The congregation as a whole pronounced (or chanted) these words as a reply to the six petitions, which were said by the celebrant. But this fact does not hinder us from understanding the meaning of these words. What were the thoughts of the people in the primitive church of the second century when at the end of the Lord's Prayer they spoke or chanted this doxology? One can see in it a relation to the sixth petition, "Deliver us from the Evil One," because the kingdom, the power, and the glory belong to God, not to the Devil, sin, death, or hell. "For" means, "This is why we ask thee to deliver us from the Evil One, since to thee belong the kingdom, the power, and the glory." Or, in other words, "Show us that thou art the King, powerful and glorious, by delivering us from the Evil One."

There is another explanation which does not necessarily exclude the first. These final words encompass the whole prayer. The thought would be thus: It is necessary for us to pray, because to thee belong the kingdom, the power, and the glory, and not to us, human beings, Christians, pious people. All that we ask of thee can be done only by thee. This is why we address ourselves to thee. The Heidelberg Catechism offers this explanation: "Thou art our King, the All-Powerful, who art able and willing to give us every benefit, in order that thy name may be glorified"—thy name and not ours or the name of Christianity or of the church.

"Amen."

It is enough to recall what Luther and the Heidelberg Catechism tell us about this. Luther affirms that it is a good thing to say "Amen"! In other words, it is a good

A Selection of
Barth's Pastoral Prayers

I

O Sovereign God! You have humbled yourself in order to exalt us. You became poor so that we might become rich. You came to us so that we can come to you. You took upon yourself our humanity in order to raise us up into eternal life. All this comes through your grace, free and unmerited; all this through your beloved Son, our Lord and Savior, Jesus Christ.

We are gathered here for prayer in the knowledge of this mystery and this wonder. We come to praise you, to proclaim and hear your word. We know that we have no strength to do so unless you make us free to lift our hearts and thoughts to you. Be present now in our midst, we pray. Through your Holy Spirit open for us the way to come to you, that we may see with our own eyes your light which has come into the world, and then in the living of our lives become your witnesses. Amen.

II

GIVE US YOUR SPIRIT (PENTECOST)

O Sovereign God, we come to you face to face, bowing before your majesty in recognition of our unworthiness and giving thanks for all the good gifts which you give us again and again for body and soul. We thank you especially for this Sunday, this holy day, on which we may ponder the fact that your dear Son, our Lord Jesus Christ, did not leave us orphaned after his return to you, but desired to be present and remain present to us through the Holy Spirit, the Comforter and Teacher who gives us life, until our Lord himself returns to us in majesty. And now, grant that we may know you truly and praise you fully in the midst of your blessings to us, that your word may be proclaimed aright and heard aright in this place and everywhere that your people call upon you. Hallow and bless our celebration of the Lord's Supper, as we share in it with one another. May your light enlighten us, your peace be among us. Amen.

III

O Sovereign God, we praise you and thank you that out of your incomprehensible mercy you did in your beloved Son humble yourself for our sakes in order to exalt us in him for your own sake. We praise you and give you thanks for your power revealed in your purpose for your people Israel and for the unbelieving nations out of which you called our ancestors. We praise you and thank you for your gracious election and calling, and for being also the God of those rejected and uncalled, and for never ceasing to care for us all in righteousness and as a father. Let us not grow weary in knowing and worshiping you in all these mysteries and thus laying hold of the word in faith, for through faith you are exalted in honor and are ready to give us even now in this life peace and joy, together with eternal blessedness.

We pray to you for your church here and in all lands: that the sleeping church might awake, that the persecuted church might be renewed in joy and confidence, that the confessing church might live not for itself but for your glory alone.

We pray to you for all who rule and hold authority throughout the whole world: for those who are good, that you would preserve them; for those who are evil, that you would convert their hearts or bring their power to an end as you see fit; for them all, that you would show yourself to them as the one whose servants they are and must remain.

We pray you to oppose all tyranny and disorder and to help all oppressed nations and persons to gain their rights.

We pray to you for the poor, the sick, the captives, the helpless, the disturbed, for all who suffer things which you alone know of. Comfort them with your presence and with the hope of your kingdom. Amen.

IV

O Sovereign God, through Jesus Christ your Son you have humbled yourself in order to exalt us. You became poor to make us rich. You suffered and died, and in so doing gave us freedom and life. And this eternal mercy and goodness displays your might and majesty as our Creator and Lord, the glory in which we praise you and in the light of which we may live all the days you give to us. For this we thank you.

And in thanking you, we can come to you aright. We are able to spread out before you all that to our understanding seems hard and perplexing and in need of your care. In your mercy remember us all and be merciful to us, now and forever, for without you we can do nothing.

Have mercy on our church on earth in its division and dispersion, its weakness and its error.

Have mercy on the old and the young, on unbelievers far and near, on the godless and the idolators who have not, or have not yet, heard your name in truth. Have mercy on the governments and the peoples of this earth, on their perplexity as they search for peace and righteousness, and also on the confusion in our human endeavors in science, nurture, and education, and on all the difficulties in so many marriages and families.

Have mercy on the countless persons who today suffer starvation, the many who are persecuted and homeless, the sick in body and soul here and in other places, the lonely, prisoners, and all those who suffer punishment at the hands of others.

Have mercy on us all in the hour of trial and the hour of death. Lord, because we believe with certainty that you have overcome, and that with you we too have already overcome, we call upon you now. Show us but the first step of the road to freedom, won at such cost. Amen.

V

O Sovereign God, it is through your inconceivable greatness that we are able to call upon you: Lord, *our* God, *our* Creator, *our* Parent, *our* Savior. In that greatness you know and love us all, you desire to be known and loved by us all, you see and guide our paths, and we all may come before you and go to be with you.

And now we pour out before you all our cares, that you may care for us; our hopes and wishes, that they may be granted not according to our will but according to *your* will; our sins, that you may forgive them; our thoughts and desires, that you may cleanse them; our whole life in these times, that you may bring us to the resurrection of all humanity and to eternal life. We remember before you all who are in this house, and also all the men and women in prison throughout the world. Be with the members of our families at home, with all who are poor, sick, hard beset, or sorrowing. Enlighten the thoughts and rule the actions of those who in our land and in all lands are responsible for law, order, and peace. Let it be day, through Jesus Christ, our Lord. Amen.

VI (Based on a prayer by Calvin)

By your judgment, Almighty God, we stand and fall. Grant that we may see our weakness and powerlessness aright, and let us remember always that you are our power and strength. Help us to let go of all trust in ourselves and in the goods of this world. Teach us to seek refuge in you, and to place confidently in your hands our present life and our eternal salvation, that we may always be yours, and give you honor. Help us learn to rest in you alone and to live in a manner pleasing to you.

You are the beginning and the end of our salvation; grant, therefore, O God, that we may be subject to you in fear and trembling and follow wherever you call us to go. Grant that we may constantly call upon you and cast our sorrows upon you, until we have finally escaped all dangers and come to that eternal peace prepared for us by the suffering, death, and resurrection of your only begotten Son. Amen.

VII

Loving heavenly Father, we give you thanks. Work now in our hearts and in what we say and do, so that we may praise you and obey you day by day; that we may do so today and, by the might of your Holy Spirit, tomorrow and the day after as well. Support us and bear us forward, each of us. This we all need, each in his or her own way. Be and remain our God and our help, for us, for all who are in this house, and also for the members of our families nearby or far away.

Remain unchanging, O God, both above and in the human actions and events of our days, so confusing and confused, oppressing and oppressive. Tell everyone and show them all that they are not lost from you, and that they cannot run from you. Show yourself everywhere as the Lord of the godly and the godless, of the wise and the foolish, of the healthy and the sick, as the Lord too of our poor church. You are ruler of Protestants, of Catholics, and of all others. Ruler of good and bad governments, of the nourished and the undernourished peoples, and especially of those who feel they must speak out and write whether for better or for worse. For you are Defender of us all, to whom we may commit ourselves, but also the Judge of us all, to whom we must answer both now and on the Last Day.

Great, holy, and merciful God, we long for your final revelation, when it will become clear to all eyes that the created world and its history and the course of all human lives were, are, and will be always in your strict and generous hand. We thank you too that we may look forward to this final revelation. All this we pray in the name of Jesus Christ, in whom you have loved, chosen, and called humanity from all eternity. Amen.

VIII

O Lord God, you are great, holy, and exalted above us and above all humankind. And now you show your greatness by not forgetting us or deserting us, and, in spite of all that condemns us, by not rejecting us. You have given us in your dear Son, Jesus Christ, nothing less than your own self and all that is yours. We thank you for the privilege of being guests at the table prepared for us by your grace for as long as we live and even for all eternity.

We bring before you now all that troubles us: our failings, errors, and exaggerations, our tribulations and sorrows, and also our rebelliousness and bitterness—our whole life and our whole heart, which you know better than we know it ourselves. We place all this in the faithful hands which you have stretched out to us in our Savior. Take us as we are; raise up those who are weak, enrich from your fullness those who are poor.

And let your companionship illumine our families and all those who are captive or who suffer need or are sick or near death. Give to those who judge, the spirit of righteousness; and to those who rule in this world, a measure of your wisdom to guide them to peace on earth. Give insight and courage to those who at home or as missionaries abroad proclaim your word.

And now we bring our petitions together as we call on you as our Savior has granted and bidden us:

Our Father . . .

Karl Barth on Prayer

I. JOHN HESSELINK

Introduction

As far as I know, Karl Barth has never been called a man of prayer. I am not thinking primarily of his personal life, for here it would be difficult to make any judgment since Barth, like Calvin, was reluctant to speak of his personal life of faith. I am referring, rather, to the fact that when one thinks about Barth's many contributions to theology, few people, including Barth specialists, would suggest that prayer was one of them. Given Barth's ambivalent feelings about pietism, one might even surmise that Barth had little interest in prayer, despite his well-known little book on the Lord's Prayer based on the catechisms of the Reformation.[1]

This impression—that Barth has little to contribute to, and was not much interested in, prayer—would appear to be confirmed by the fact that three of the earlier comprehensive studies of Barth's theology, viz., those by G. C. Berkouwer,[2] Hans Urs von Balthasar,[3] and Herbert Hartwell,[4] have no reference to prayer in their indexes. This is strange in view of the fact that, in addition to his little book on the Lord's Prayer, Barth had fairly lengthy treatments of prayer in two earlier volumes of the *Church Dogmatics*, in III/3,[5] in the context of the providence of God, and in III/4[6] in his ethics of creation.

There is even less justification for omitting this as a major motif in Barth's theology. For in his "swan song," *Evangelical Theology: An Introduction*,[7] prayer is one of the topics under the heading "Theological Work"; and the posthumously published fragment, *The Christian Life*,[8] is devoted almost entirely to the first two petitions of the Lord's Prayer. As a result, more attention has been paid to Barth's treatment of prayer in recent years,[9] but it is still hardly worthy of the space Barth has devoted to this subject in his writings—over 540 pages in all!

Hence it may be fair to conclude that having written so much and so passionately about this subject, Barth was indeed a man of prayer as well as a notable theologian of prayer.

Prayer and Theology

Some, but by no means all, theologians have devoted a chapter in their dogmatics or systematic theologies to prayer, but no one to my knowledge relates prayer so intimately to the doing of the theology. At the head of his first dogmatics Barth cited the prayer of Thomas Aquinas, "Merciful God, I pray thee to grant me, if it please thee, ardour to desire thee, diligence to seek thee, wisdom to know thee, and skill to speak to the glory of thy name. Amen."[10] Then Barth comments:

> If there is any mortally dangerous undertaking on earth, any undertaking in which we have reason not only at the beginning but also in the middle and at the end to take the last resort of invoking the name

of the Most High, then it is that of a *summa theolog-ica*, a dogmatics, and I must add that in our day and our situation such a prayer will have to be made out of materially much deeper distress and perplexity than in the time of Thomas.[11]

Barth does not speak this explicitly in his later *Church Dogmatics* about the necessity of prayer in doing theology, but at the end of his career he made the same point in his *Evangelical Theology: An Introduction*. In his discussion of theological work the first chapter is on prayer. Again he stresses that no one can undertake the task of theology in one's own strength. "Precisely the knowledge that by our own power nothing at all can be accomplished, allows and requires courageous action."[12] Therefore, "the first and basic act of theological work is *prayer*." It is also study and service as well as an act of love. But, echoing his comments in the *Göttingen Dogmatics*, he notes that "theological work does not merely begin with prayer and is not merely accompanied by it; in its totality it is peculiar and charac-teristic of theology that it can be performed only in the act of prayer . . . without prayer there can be no theological work."[13] For Barth, "Where theology is concerned, the rule *Ora et labora!* is valid under all circumstances—pray and work!"[14] Since the task of theology is a reflection on the revelation of the living God, theology, through a rational inquiry, will also be an activity of wonder, love, and praise. Hence all true theology will not only begin with prayer, but will be pervaded by prayer. Those who are familiar with his theology will recognize that Barth, all of his theological acumen notwithstanding, always bowed before the mystery of his subject matter, the object of his faith, and thus was gladly and by necessity a theologian of prayer.

The Place of Prayer in Barth's Theology

What may come as a surprise to some people is that Barth discusses prayer primarily in the context of ethics; and unlike many theologians, ethics for Barth is not an independent subject separated from the traditional loci of dogmatics, but is an integral element of dogmatics. Though Barth did write a separate ethics early in his teaching career—in Münster in 1928–29[15]—these lectures in many ways are a "first draft" of the ethical sections of his later *Church Dogmatics*.[16] Already here in this first attempt at a theological ethics there are extensive discussions of prayer. What makes Barth's theological approach distinctive, however, is not only his treating prayer in the context of ethics, but his incorporating ethics into his doctrine of creation (*CD* III) and his doctrine of reconciliation (*CD* IV).[17] Had he completed the *Church Dogmatics* with the doctrine of redemption (vol. 5), i.e., eschatology, he might have taken up the subject of prayer—in the context of special ethics a fourth time! As it is, he devotes approximately 250 pages to the first two petitions of the Lord's Prayer in the incomplete lecture fragments of IV/4 entitled *The Christian Life*. Imagine what kind of tome IV/4 might have been if he had completed it! (The first part of *CD* IV is on baptism, the *foundation* of the Christian life;[18] the second part, prayer, of which the Lord's Prayer is the model, is the center or *continuation* of the faith; and the third part, the Lord's Supper—never written— represents the *renewal* of the Christian faith.)

The basic question, however, is: In what sense is prayer, and in particular the Lord's Prayer, central to Christian ethics? The answer, in short, is that in special ethics we have to do with the command of God, and God has commanded us to pray. In Barth's doctrine of creation this subject is subsumed under the heading of "Freedom before God." This has three foci: the Lord's Day, confession, and prayer and all three are "commanded activities."[19] "The real basis of prayer is man's freedom before God, the God-given permission to pray, which, because it is given by God, becomes a command and order and therefore a necessity."[20]

This is how Barth introduces the subject of prayer in his ethics of God the Creator. When he takes up the ethics of God the Reconciler some twenty years later, the *leitmotif* is the command of Psalm 50:15: "Call upon me," for "the living of the Christian life in obedience to that command is understood as an invocation of God."[21] However, that command does not come from any God but the God and Father of Jesus Christ, who "enables, invites, and summons" us to invoke God as Father. Hence the obedience that is commanded of us is grounded in God's grace.[22]

Barth's Theology of Prayer

Thus far we have skirted the key issue of what is prayer as such? For all the complexity and expansiveness of Barth's many discussions of prayer, a surprisingly simple initial answer can be given: prayer is first and foremost petition. In other words, "prayer, or praying, is simply asking." This "controls and includes everything else one may say about prayer."[23] Barth recognizes other dimensions of prayer, such as confession and thanksgiving, but throughout his writings on prayer, this motif is dominant.

This conviction, stated early in his *Church Dogmatics* (in III/3), comes to be the ruling theme of the final fragments of his ethics of reconciliation entitled *The Christian Life*. Here life in Christ is discussed under the rubric of invocation, or calling upon God, a key text being Psalm 50:15: "Call upon me." We understand this command, says Barth, "to be the basic meaning of every divine command, and we regard invocation as the basic meaning of all human obedience."[24] Clearly invocation, as understood by Barth in this context, involves far more than simply calling upon God in prayer from time to time. It is that, for "it is the movement in which the children [of God] bring themselves to the attention of their Father and cry to him in recollection, clearly reminding themselves that he is their Father and they are his children." But invocation has the more comprehensive meaning that "the whole life" of Christians becomes an invocation that aims at the renewal and actualization of the believer's relationship with God.[25]

However, even when petition is more broadly conceived as invocation in this sense, the question can still be raised whether defining prayer as primarily petition, "simply asking" God for that which we need, doesn't seem like a self-centered understanding of prayer.[26] Shouldn't prayer be understood first as a glorifying of God, the "chief part of gratitude" (Heidelberg Catechism, Q. 116)? Does not the Lord's Prayer begin with the hallowing of God's name, the coming of the kingdom, and the realization of God's will? Barth, of course, is fully aware of this, and does ample justice to the first three petitions of the Lord's Prayer that deal with the glory of God.[27]

Moreover, Barth understands asking God in prayer as "the most genuine act of praise and thanksgiving, and therefore worship." Praying thus is also an act of penitence, for "by coming before God as one who asks," the believer "magnifies God and abases himself."[28] In the act of confessing one's sins in prayer, "perhaps the very highest honor that God claims from man and man can pay him is that man should seek and ask and accept at God's hands, not just something, but everything that he needs."[29]

Citing several New Testament texts, Barth notes that the invocation of God as Father is "a crying," according to Romans 8:33, "a sighing," according to Colossians 3:16 and Ephesians 5:19, and "a singing" and a "rejoicing" according to Luke 10:21. "Materially, it is a thanksgiving, a praising, and above all a praying and interceding. . . ."[30] To call upon God is always a work of obedience and faith on the part of the children of God. This means especially that "they are to thank God and to thank him again and again" for all that he has done for them and will do for them in the "freely given gift" of his Son.[31]

One could cite much more evidence to show that Barth recognizes all the dimensions of prayer—praise and thanksgiving, confession, and intercession, as well as petition and "simply asking." But this is not the real point. Barth has a special apologetic or polemic reason for emphasizing prayer as petition. In a warning that is prophetic and far more relevant now than when he first wrote it, Barth points out the danger of thinking of prayer as basically meditation which has no concrete substance. There are, he notes in passing, "certain theories of prayer which finally amount to little more than an understanding of prayer as the highest form of religious or Christian self-edification, a living and fruitful dialogue between the Christian and himself."[32]

These words were penned by Barth more than forty years ago. They are even more relevant in our time when New Age spiritualities flourish in which their adherents are urged to meditate upon the god or the goddess within. Barth reiterates his concern about this understanding of prayer in his final lectures of the *Church Dogmatics*. Here he writes in a similar vein and criticizes those "spiritual" types who think of prayer as a form of self-help and a "kind of alleviation, uplift, and purification that a person might achieve on his own when engaging in a lofty monologue as though he were speaking with God as with another person" (translation emended).[33]

Another reason for Barth's strong rejection of any concept of prayer that restricts it to the subjective sphere is that it negates any expectation of prayer being answered. Here, again, Barth flies in the face of much academic treatment of prayer that is skeptical about any concrete results in response to petitionary prayer.[34] Psychologist David Myers, for example, affirms that "through prayer we thank and praise God, we humbly confess our sin and acknowledge our dependence on God's grace, we express our concerns, we experience our relationship with God, and we seek inward peace and the strength to live as God's people."[35] This is fine and good. But note what is missing here: the note that Barth sounds so emphatically—that it is right and proper to ask God for specific things and to expect an answer, although not necessarily in ways we can anticipate. Barth's treatment of this subject is very nuanced, for here we encounter the issue of the sovereignty of God and human freedom, but it is nonetheless bold and emphatic. "There can be no place," he writes, "for all the pious and impious arguments against the permissibility and possibility of asking in prayer."[36]

Barth takes seriously Jesus' teachings about prayer in this regard: "Ask, and it shall be given you; seek and you shall find; knock and it shall be opened unto you" (Matt. 7:7).[37] Here we have the God "who lets himself be spoken to, who comes afresh in his free grace to those, who moved by his free grace, come to him who gives when his children ask obediently, who satisfies their seeking by letting them find, who accepts their knocking and opens to them (Matt. 7:7)."[38] Hence, no request is too small or too great: "No little tear is too small before him (P. Gerhardt)."[39] "No little hands, stretched out or folded before him, are too dirty to achieve something with him." In short, "no request by any child of God is not fulfilled by God the Father." For "the only prayer that can be unanswered is prayer that is uncertain of an answer, so that it is not calling upon the true God."[40] For prayer to be effective, it must be offered confidently, boldly, expectantly—but this has "nothing whatever to do with human presumption."[41]

Having cited these bold, unequivocal statements, it is now necessary to nuance these remarks lest one conclude that Barth's view of petitionary prayer is simplistic and ignores some serious theological implications.

First, these latter remarks about prayer as petition are made in the context of prayer as praise and thanksgiving.[42] Not to ask God for things is an act of ingratitude. Worse, it is a sign of arrogance, for it suggests that we don't need God's help in our daily life, not to mention times of crisis and loss.[43]

Second, hearing precedes asking. "It is the basis of it."[44] Prayer is a response to God's goodness and grace in Jesus Christ. He is the "one great gift" and at the same time the "one great answer," for in and through him Christians are commanded and invited to make their requests known to God.[45]

This leads to the third point: that true prayer is offered in the name and mediation of Jesus Christ (see John 14:13; 16:23). Prayer "in the name of Jesus is prayer which we expect to be heard only . . . because God has loved and loves and will love the one who offers it as a lost sinner in Jesus Christ because Jesus Christ has come between this one and God. . . ."[46] Christ is the great Suppliant; that is, in making our supplications, we are "simply taking the divine gift and answer as it is already given to us in Jesus Christ." So he is "the first and proper suppliant."[47] Moreover, Christ, along with the Holy Spirit, is the great intercessor. "The Spirit helps us in our weakness, for we do not know how to pray as we ought" (Rom. 8:26). "Both Jesus Christ with his prayer and also the Holy Spirit with 'unutterable groanings' is our Mediator and Intercessor."[48]

Fourth, presupposed in the efficaciousness of petitionary prayer is the faith and obedience of the one who prays. For "without faith the Christian cannot pray," but at the same time "the prayer of the Christian to God is the basic act of obedience entered in faith."[49] Christian action is impossible apart from the obedience of faith, and that in turn is nourished and sustained by prayer. In a lovely summary statement, Barth simply states the relationship.

> When the Christian wishes to act obediently, what else can he do but that which he does in prayer: render to God praise and thanksgiving; spread himself before God in his weakness and sin; reach out to Him with all that impels him; commend himself to [God] who is his only help; and again, this time truly render to Him praise and thanksgiving. This is Christian obedience *in nuce*.[50]

Fifth, as we have seen, Barth is unhesitating in affirming that God answers our prayers. But God does so "according to his own good pleasure and purpose and to his own glory" as well as in the "best interests" of the believer. Not only that, God does "far more abundantly than all that we ask or think" (Eph. 3:20).[51] So God hears Christians "superabundantly" and "gives place to their invocation in an infinitely better sense than that in which even they can perform it."[52] They can be sure of an answer, and the answer will be "more or less congruent" with their requests. Sometimes they will be "fairly literally fulfilled," but Christians cannot always "expect and demand that the glory of the hearing should consist in the congruence of the divine fulfilling with the limited form of the asking. . . ." Instead, they must accept "a fulfillment that is a transformation of the prayer itself." For when God hears a prayer he "transforms" it so that it "will truly be to his own glory and their salvation."[53]

Finally, we come to the most difficult and intriguing question of all in relation to any theology of prayer. If God does indeed answer our prayers, to what extent is God moved and changed by them? Here we encounter again the age-old question of God's sovereignty and human freedom. Process theologians, and more recently "free will theists" (openness of God) theologians have challenged the classical theistic position represented by Augustine, Aquinas, Calvin, and most modern Reformed theologians, including Barth.[54] However, it turns out that Barth is more flexible and open than his critics give him credit for, although he will uphold steadfastly the sovereignty of God even in regard to prayer and providence.

On the one hand, Barth does not hesitate to say that God not only listens to our prayers, he acts. And "he does not act in the same way whether we pray or not." For "prayer exerts an influence upon God's action, even upon his existence."[55] Barth states the matter even more forcibly in his final lectures. Here he writes that God "does not despise" the feeble, flawed, and inadequate requests of his children. "He lets himself be touched and moved by [them]."[56]

Not only that, prayer "puts us in rapport with God and permits us to collaborate with him."[57] Elsewhere, Barth speaks of Christians as "partners" with God in response to their calling upon him in prayer. God in his free grace "makes [believers] his partners and himself their partner" in such a way that he forges a "close link between their invocation and his answering, their action and his."[58]

> When God's children invoke him as Father, this is in no sense a venture, a mere gesture, a shot in the dark, an experiment or a gamble. They do this as those who have a part in the history in which God is their partner and they are his partners, in which they are liberated for this action and summoned to it, in which there is also given to them the promise of his corresponding action and therefore of his hearing.[59]

This kind of language has an Arminian ring that is reinforced when Barth speaks elsewhere of a "real cooperation" in doing God's will. In this context, Barth proceeds to make an interesting contrast. "In obedience," he says, "the Christian is the servant, in faith he is the child, but in prayer, as the servant and the child, he is the friend of God called to the side of God *and at the side of God, living and ruling and reigning with him*" (emphasis mine).[60] In prayer, Christians enjoy "a genuine and actual share in the lordship of God."[61]

However, this is only one side of the matter. Thus far I have deliberately omitted those passages where Barth speaks out of the other side of his mouth. However, Barth also points out that

> the fact that God yields to human petitions, that he alters his intentions and follows the bent of our prayers, is not a sign of weakness. In his own majesty

and in the splendor of his might, he has willed and yet wills it so. He desires to be the God who has been flesh in Jesus Christ. Therein lies his glory, his omnipotence. He does not then impair himself by yielding to our prayer; on the contrary, it is in so doing that he shows his greatness.[62]

Barth does not hesitate to use one of the classical attributes of God such as his immutability, an attribute much criticized of late by Process and Openness of God theologians, as well as by those who make much of the God who suffers. We can still speak of God's immutability, Barth believes, but not in the Greek sense that God is not affected, moved, and even "determined" by the course of world events. All this notwithstanding, Barth can still affirm God's sovereignty in no uncertain terms.

God is not free and immutable in the sense that he is the prisoner of his own resolve and will and action, that he must always be above as the Lord of all things and of all occurrence. He is free and immutable as the living God, as the God who wills to converse with the creature, and to allow himself to be determined by it in this relationship. His sovereignty is so great that it embraces both the possibility, and, as it is exercised, the actuality, that the creature can cooperate in his overruling. There is no creaturely freedom which can limit or compete with the sole sovereignty and efficacy of God. But permitted by God, and indeed willed and created by him, there is the freedom of the friends of God concerning whom he has determined that without abandoning the helm for a moment he will still allow himself to be determined by them.[63]

This borders on stark paradox, but Barth prefers to see this freedom of God—freedom of human tension as "the heart and mystery" of world occurrence. Whenever a Christian prays, there is what Barth calls "a creaturely movement." However, "concealed within the creaturely movement . . . there moves the finger and hand and scepter of the God who rules the world." The subjective element—our impotent asking as we come to God with empty hands in prayer—"conceals and contains and actualizes the most objective of all things, the lordship of the One who as King of Israel and King of the kingdom of grace holds all things in his own hands, and directs everything that occurs in this world for the best: *per Jesum Christum, Dominum nostrum.*"[64]

There is thus a certain "reciprocity" between the freedom of God and the freedom God has granted believers by his grace—they are "not marionettes who move only at his will"[65]—so that he can speak of them as "partners." But their "codetermination of the divine action implies no limitation of the divine sovereignty. It only means that God's sovereignty is not that of a tyrant."[66] God takes seriously the service of his children, but "he, and not they, decides how and to what extent he does so." He "never lets the reins slip from his fingers."[67] Thus, God's sovereignty is "not an abstract and absolute sovereignty but the relative and concrete sovereignty of his free and real and effective grace to people in Jesus Christ and of his real and effective Holy Spirit who truly liberates them. It is very proper for him, then, to let his action be codetermined by his children who have been freed for obedience to him."[68]

This type of reasoning may be difficult for some to follow, let alone accept. As George Hunsinger has noted, some people have charged Barth with incoherence in his presentation of divine sovereignty and human freedom.

Hunsinger's response is that this kind of "double agency" must be seen in the light of the Chalcedonian handling of the natures of Christ. Prayer, as Barth explains it, represents "the mysterious conception of this double agency" at its very epitome and height."[69] Only thus can one avoid the Scylla of determinism on the part of God and the Charybdis of indeterminism on the part of humans or some form of dialectical identity.[70] Beyond this reason cannot go. We must bow before the mystery.

The Criteria for True Prayer

In his treatment of prayer in the ethics of creation (*CD* III/4), Barth, similarly to Calvin, lists five "criteria of true prayer."[71] These can be dealt with briefly because much of the material covered here has already been discussed in other contexts.

The first is that "a man prays because he is permitted to do so by God, because he may pray, and because this very permission has become a command."[72] Here "we stand before the innermost center of the covenant between God and man which is the meaning of creation, God's gracious will."[73] Prayer, therefore, finds its basis in the command of the gracious God, not in human need.

The second criterion is that prayer is "decisively petition."[74] This has been discussed at some length above, so here it is only necessary to add that this includes thanksgiving, penitence, and worship. (Note Barth's order here.) Also, though we are unworthy, we can pray frankly and fearlessly because God cleanses the requests that come from our unclean lips.[75]

The third criterion has to do with the question of the relation of the individual who prays to the "we" referred to in the opening of the Lord's Prayer: "*Our* Father, who art in heaven." The "we" refers to those who belong to Jesus Christ, "who has summoned, invited and claimed them, whom he has summoned to pray with him." However, "we," who so pray, pray not only for ourselves but for that world which does not yet believe. Moreover, even when we pray for ourselves we do so as members of a Christian community.[76]

Fourth, true prayer is "prayer which is sure of a hearing."[77] The only question here is not whether God will answer our prayers and act on them, but whether we will pray with this assurance. After citing a number of biblical passages that speak confidently about what believers can expect in prayer and a similar confidence on the part of the Reformers, Barth concludes that "this assurance is unconditionally demanded."[78]

The fifth criterion has to do with the form of prayer in ethics. Here again Barth discusses the relation of the individual to the community and vice versa. Whether private or public prayer, as petition it will have the character of intercession. Here Barth cites a number of biblical passages that have as their common theme that we are to pray for each other; the chief example of this is Jesus' high priestly prayer.[79]

Then Barth makes a number of practical observations:

1. Whether private or public prayer, "both are subject to a certain discipline." A degree of freedom is possible but it must be within a certain discipline and order.[80]
2. There may be a time and place when silent prayer is appropriate, "but there can hardly be prayer which does not shape indefinite thoughts and words." Barth, obviously, is no mystic, for he adds that on the whole, wordless prayer cannot be regarded as true prayer.[81]

3. Since we need to pray often and cannot always find the right words, there is "a relative legitimacy and necessity of formulated prayer." The Lord's Prayer takes pride of place here. Other formal prayers can be helpful but ideally one should generally pray in one's own words. However, Barth concedes the validity of the rule: "Better according to a form than not at all."[82]

4. In prayer, especially in public worship, brevity is a virtue. Extemporaneous prayers are all right if, like Calvin's prayers after his sermons and biblical lectures, they are "short and good."[83]

5. In view of human weakness, it is probably best to have definite times and hours of prayer. Barth points with approval to the practice of grace before meals and "the pious custom of morning and evening prayer [which] has a solid basis in what is on the biblical view of things the meaningful alternation of light and darkness." Here, as elsewhere in those matters, Barth is fairly flexible and cautious against making absolute rules. However, those people who reject such disciplines "must continually ask themselves whether they really do have serious reasons or whether the secret of their refusal to be bound is not simply a blatant or more subtle slovenliness."[84]

6. On the other hand, prayers should "take place in man's free hearty and spontaneous obedience." One of the worst things that can happen is when prayers are mechanical and merely serve to salve one's conscience. Here Barth is critical of the Roman Catholic discipline of prayer as it developed in the medieval church.[85]

7. Barth recognizes the problem of prayer in worship where on the one hand the pastoral prayer should be

disciplined and congregational, and on the other hand should be "free, hearty, and spontaneous." The problem is especially acute in larger congregations where there is less possibility for freedom. Ministers who pray freely must not rely on instant inspiration. Here Barth is torn, for as much as he abhors thoughtless, rambling prayers so common in evangelical tradition, he is even more unhappy about the reading of prayers from ancient liturgies which do not speak the language or express the concerns of a modern congregation. Barth is obviously not a high churchman! Perhaps the best solution, he concludes, "is for the minister to make 'extemporary' prayer no less an object of serious and careful preparation than the proclamation of the Word of God. . . ."[86]

The responsibility here, however, is not just that of the minister. Congregations must also face up to this question and take it seriously, for it is "a burning question which is not merely a matter of taste and judgment but of life and death." For Barth, the nature and form of prayer should not simply be a concern of practical theology but a major issue for all of Christendom.[87] In all our efforts at church renewal and church growth in North America, of all the proposals that are made, one rarely, if ever, hears this concern. Here, as in several other areas of church life, Barth may well be a prophet for our time.

The Lord's Prayer

It would be hard to match the enthusiasm Barth has for the Lord's Prayer and the theological depth of his analysis of it. One angle of Barth's vision is found in the brief semipopular treatment of the Lord's Prayer that is made available above.[88]

The Lord's Prayer, for Barth, is fundamental for the church and the life of faith because "it is a breviary of the whole gospel" (Tertullian), "the essence of prayer."[89] For "it invites us in a unique fashion to apply the old adage that the law of prayer is the law of faith."[90] Above all, "when a man prays the Lord's Prayer, externally at least his praying is more surely carried, led and protected by the prayer of Jesus Christ himself, and more surely set in the fellowship of the prayer of Christendom, than when he goes his own way as a praying individual."[91] In regard to the former, i.e., when an individual prays the Lord's Prayer, Barth likes to cite the phrase from Calvin to the effect that when we pray "we pray as it were by [Christ's] mouth."[92]

In the first three petitions, "we," i.e., the Christian community, are "invited and summoned . . . to take up the cause of God and actively to participate in it with our asking."[93] For God is not a solitary God who desires to work and rule alone, but wills that his cause should not only be his but also ours, but in a way appropriate to the fact that he is the creator and we are creatures.[94]

The other important thing to note in the first three petitions is the corporate character of the prayer—"*our* Father," not mine—and the fact that unworthy sinners can address God as "our *Father*" because we come in the name and grace of Jesus Christ.[95] Both these points have been mentioned above.

The last three petitions "are the inversion and consequence of the first three." Before we were invited to espouse God's cause, his name and kingdom and will. Now we ask God to espouse and participate in our cause, the need for food, forgiveness, and protection from the

Evil One. Our cause is secure, not because of our faithfulness in prayer and action, but because God in Jesus Christ had made it his own.[96] Ultimately, however, the two causes are one in Jesus Christ.[97]

Or, to put the matter more simply, "In the first three petitions our prayer is a sort of conversation with the heavenly Father. It is like a sigh. We are dazzled by the grandeur of what occupies us." Whereas, with the last three petitions we come to prayer properly speaking.[98] Here prayer becomes "explicit, direct, and imperative."[99] However, it is precisely in our asking that we acknowledge our dependence on God and thereby glorify him.

Other scholars have also written about Barth's views on prayer and the Lord's Prayer.[100] But the comment by Saliers is apt:

> Barth's own intense understanding of the Lord's Prayer from the inside out, so to speak, unfolds a key aspect of his whole theological undertaking. While the task appears to be an informal exposition and posing of a 'theology of prayer,' it manifests the much more elemental feature of Barth's work, an entire theology oriented toward prayer and worship.[101]

A Prayer of Barth's

Barth's pastoral prayers, like those of Calvin, which he admired, are brief, but unlike Calvin's, were apparently not spontaneous, for they are appended to his later sermons.[102] A few of these prayers have also been added to the second edition of *Prayer*. I would like to conclude with one of those prayers.

O Sovereign God! You have humbled yourself in order to exalt us. You became poor so that we might become rich. You came to us so that we can come to you. You took upon yourself our humanity in order to raise us up into eternal life. All this comes through your grace, free and unmerited; all this through your beloved Son, our Lord and Savior, Jesus Christ.

We are gathered here for prayer in the knowledge of this mystery and this wonder. We come to praise you, to proclaim and hear your word. We know that we have no strength to do so unless you make us free to lift our hearts and thoughts to you. Be present now in our midst, we pray. Through your Holy Spirit open for us the way to come to you, that we may see with our own eyes your light which has come into the world, and then in the living of our lives become your witnesses. Amen.[103]

Freedom to Pray

Karl Barth's Theology of Prayer

DANIEL L. MIGLIORE

Introduction

There is abundant evidence of a new interest in spirituality and prayer in the church today. After a period of intense activism that sometimes marginalized or even replaced serious concern for worship and prayer, theology and ministry are turning their attention to the deep spiritual foundations of Christian life without which the call to action so easily leads to burnout or cynicism. There is both real promise and possible danger in this development. The promise is that Christians will learn "to drink from their own wells"[1] as they face the social, cultural, moral, and religious crises of our time. The danger is that interest in spirituality may become a new fad driven more by popular culture and market forces than by a biblically grounded understanding and practice of prayer.

Of the resources available to the church for serious reflection on the place of prayer in Christian life, ministry, and theology, the work of Karl Barth is among the richest. No other theologian of the twentieth century took prayer more seriously or developed a more extensive theology of prayer than did Barth. In this paper I will first sketch the central themes of Barth's theology of prayer and then summarize his description of the significance of prayer for theological work. With this background I will then consider Barth's understanding of the act of prayer as a clue to the right understanding of the relationship of divine sovereignty and human freedom. In the final section I will contend that we must go further than Barth did in including the freedom to lament and protest within the freedom to pray.

The Central Themes of Barth's Theology of Prayer

In the lectures given during his only trip to the United States, Barth challenged his hearers not to become champions of past or present theological schools, whether Thomism, Calvinism, or Barthianism, but to develop instead a theology of freedom.[2] The motif of freedom— the freedom of God and the freedom of the covenant partners of God—appears everywhere in the *Church Dogmatics*. Not surprisingly, this theme also marks his theology of prayer: for Barth, prayer is the quintessential act of human freedom before God.

1. Barth considers and rejects two standard answers to the question, Why is prayer necessary? The first attempts to ground the necessity of prayer in human need. We must pray, so this answer would say, because we are weak and needy, and we are thus moved to seek help from beyond ourselves. In Barth's judgment, however, our needs do not necessarily teach us to pray. They might just as easily teach us to curse, or scoff, or become resigned, or work all the harder to satisfy our needs by ourselves. A second answer to the question, Why is prayer necessary? is that we turn to God in prayer because God is the source of all blessings. If the first answer is based on a general anthro-

pology, the second answer is based on a general idea of God. According to Barth, the attempt to ground the necessity of prayer in an abstract conception of God as the source of all good is no more compelling than the effort to base it in a general theory of human neediness. The idea of God as the source of all good, far from providing a firm basis of prayer, might just as well lead to the conclusion that since God knows what we need and is able to supply all that we lack or desire, any attempt on our part to influence God would be superfluous and inappropriate.[3]

So why pray? For Barth the basis of prayer can be nothing other than the will of God, realized in Jesus Christ, that human creatures be the free covenant partners of God. In prayer human beings are permitted and commanded to come to God freely with their desires and requests. "The real basis of prayer is man's freedom before God, the God-given permission to pray which, because it is given by God, becomes a command and order and therefore a necessity."[4] As chosen partners and coworkers with God, we are invited, permitted, and commanded to pray.

While largely in agreement with Luther that prayer is based on the command of God, Barth emphasizes that this command is never to be understood as an abstract divine fiat. It is the freely gracious God who summons us to prayer. In prayer we turn to the God who has graciously drawn near to us.[5] Before we speak to God, God has already spoken to us. This is the point of Barth's claim that God is the real initiator of prayer, that God's action precedes our action, that there is always a hearing that precedes the asking of prayer.[6]

Thus the necessity of prayer according to Barth is to be found not in human need, nor in divine majesty, nor in an abstract divine command, but in God's gracious invitation and humanity's God-given freedom to pray. Only if we begin with God's concrete address to humanity above all in Jesus Christ are we able to rightly grasp the necessity of prayer. Prayer is simply "the first available use of the freedom" that has been given to us in Christ.[7]

2. If prayer is necessary because God permits and commands us to pray as those called to life in communion with and in service of God, for Barth prayer is centrally petition: asking, wishing, desiring, expecting.[8] Of course, Barth allows that prayer is other things as well: it is also adoration, thanksgiving, praise, and confession. But unlike Schleiermacher, who saw the prayer of thanksgiving and acceptance of the divine world government as the essence of Christian prayer,[9] Barth identifies the "center" of prayer as petition.[10] He points to the fact that the Lord's Prayer is simply a "string of petitions."[11] By arguing that petition is the center of prayer, Barth not only underscores the fact that we come to God with empty hands; he also emphasizes that we are summoned to pray in freedom. Understanding prayer as centrally petition assures that "the real man comes before God in prayer,"[12] that we do not have to hide any anxiety or desire in prayer. "All masks and camouflages may and must fall away" in the free act of genuine prayer.[13]

While we are to "come as we are" in prayer with all our anxiety, passion, and egoism, our praying will, of course, always stand in need of being ordered and purified.[14] Guided by the Lord's Prayer, our petitions will not be just any sort of asking. In the first three petitions of the Lord's Prayer, Christians pray for the honoring of God, the coming of God's reign, the doing of God's will; in the final three petitions they pray for daily bread, forgiveness of sins, and protection from evil. This order, Barth contends, is of great significance. Only as we first plead for the purposes of God to prevail can we properly plead for the fulfillment of our own needs and those of the church and the whole creation.

According to Barth, then, the appropriate response of humanity to God's gracious initiative is simply a life of invocation, calling on God freely in all circumstances. Invocation is the "normal action" of the free human creature in the covenant of grace that corresponds to the freely gracious action of God.[15]

3. In line with his characteristic christocentric emphasis, prayer for Barth is a *participation in the praying of Jesus Christ*. He is the supreme pray-er, the great suppliant, "the first and proper Subject of prayer" (emphasis added).[16] As the Son of God, Jesus is the divine gift and answer to human asking; as the Son of man he is the true human petitioner.[17] Representative of our true humanity, Jesus Christ "is only and altogether a Suppliant."[18] He intercedes on our behalf, petitioning on behalf of those who cannot and will not ask for themselves.[19] Thus when Christians pray to God in the name of Christ, their asking is enclosed in his asking; their petition is a "repetition of his petition."[20] In their petitionary prayer Christians participate not only in the prophetic and priestly but also in the kingly office of Christ. "Christian prayer is participation in Jesus Christ; participation, basically, in the grace which is revealed and active in Him, in the Son of God; and then only, and on this basis, participation in the asking of the Son of Man."[21] For Barth our freedom to pray is formed and disciplined by our participation in Jesus Christ.

Because our prayer is a participation in the prayer of Jesus Christ, it is sure of God's hearing. In Jesus Christ we are bound up from eternity with God, and God has bound Godself from eternity with us. Hence, "When we pray to

God we have Him on our side from the very outset, and we for our part stand on His side from the very outset, so that from the very outset we must be certain that He hears our prayer."[22]

4. For Barth Christian prayer is not individualistic prayer but fundamentally "common prayer."[23] Prayer is essentially a communal act. "Although he prays for himself as an individual, [the Christian] does not pray private prayers."[24] "Praying for himself . . . he prays with and for all other Christians, because he prays for the service and work of the community; and in so doing he prays for all men."[25] In correspondence with the prayer of Jesus Christ, the petitions of the Christian will be primarily intercession. "True private and public prayer will always have this particularly in common, that as petition they will have the character of intercession."[26] The prayers of the community are representative on behalf of all humanity and the whole creation; they give voice to the groaning of all creation.[27] Barth often stresses the communal and inclusive character of the Lord's Prayer. The "we" of the Lord's Prayer "are the members of this community, and behind them, not praying but groaning together with them, all men and all creatures."[28]

5. Prayer for Barth is the primary Christian action and thus an essential ingredient in all Christian witness and activity. Prayer and Christian ethics are inseparable. Prayer is "the most intimate and effective form of Christian action. All other work . . . is Christian work . . . only to the extent that it derives from prayer, and that it has in prayer its true and original form."[29] Barth notes that the most active workers, thinkers, and fighters in the divine service have also been the most active in prayer. He thus agrees with the classical theological rule *ora et labora*, "pray and work," but understands it to mean not that

prayer comes chronologically before work and is afterward incidental to it, but that prayer is constitutive to all faithful Christian action. Barth highlights this point in his discussion of the basic forms of Christian ministry. He identifies six forms of speech ministry (praise, preaching, instruction, evangelization, mission, and theology) and six forms of action ministry (prayer, care of souls, exemplary Christian life, service, prophetic action, and establishing fellowship). Remarkable is Barth's location of prayer as the first form of action ministry. "Prayer is a basic element in the whole action of the whole community."[30] "The community prays as it works. And in praying it works."[31] Barth thus describes prayer as the prototypical form of Christian action. In prayer the community becomes "an active partner in the covenant which God has established."[32]

6. Finally, Barth speaks of a definite discipline of prayer. While he does not make this a primary focus, it is nevertheless a basic component of his theology of prayer. He resists, of course, every utilitarian reduction of prayer, whether to extol its usefulness in achieving some social program, forming Christian character, or promoting personal piety. He is especially critical of all emphases on spiritual exercises that tend to make prayer a form of mental and spiritual hygiene. Prayer, he writes, is not "an exercise in the cultivation of the soul or spirit, i.e., the attempt to intensify and deepen ourselves, to purify and cleanse ourselves inwardly, to attain clarity and self-control, and finally to set ourselves on a good footing and in agreement with the deity by this preparation."[33] Such exercises, Barth argues, have nothing to do with genuine prayer in which we are mere suppliants and have nothing to offer to God. Still, he insists that "some sort of discipline and order cannot be absent from true prayer."[34] Prayer as an

exercise of Christian freedom is a formed, disciplined freedom. Thus, while a discipline of prayer cannot be imposed arbitrarily, our freedom to pray "will continually give rise to relative and concrete obligations."[35] Barth mentions regular participation in common prayer, morning and evening prayers, and prayers at meals as well-founded disciplines even if they cannot be mechanically mandated. Barth's fullest discussion of the discipline of prayer as an act of Christian freedom is found in his reflections on the importance of prayer in theological work, and to that topic we now turn.

Prayer and Theology

Although Barth considers prayer to be indispensable to every aspect of Christian life, he is especially attentive to its essential role in the work of theology. Prayer is "the attitude without which there can be no dogmatic work."[36] Discussing the relationship of prayer and theology in the first volume of the *Church Dogmatics*, Barth notes that Anselm cast his famous proof of the existence of God in the *Proslogion* in the form of a prayer; that Aquinas set a prayer for assistance at the beginning of his *Summa Theologiae*; and that David Hollaz, an eighteenth-century Lutheran theologian, transformed each doctrinal locus of theology into a *suspirium*, in which talk about God becomes explicit address to God.[37]

What is at stake for Barth in insisting on the importance of prayer for theology is whether theological inquiry will be a genuinely free science or whether it will be bound to some worldview, ideology, or set of pre-understandings. Prayer for Barth is, of course, no guarantee of successful theological work. Nevertheless, "Prayer can be the recognition that we accomplish nothing by our intentions, even though they be intentions to pray. Prayer can be the expression of our human willing of the will of God. Prayer can signify that for good or evil man justifies God and not himself. Prayer can be the human answer to the divine hearing already granted, the epitome of the true faith which we cannot assume of ourselves."[38] While prayer is no magic wand, "It is hard to see how else there can be successes in this work but on the basis of divine correspondence to this human attitude: 'Lord, I believe; help thou mine unbelief.'"[39]

In *Evangelical Theology*, written in the last decade of his life, Barth returns to the theme of the intimate relationship of theology and prayer. "The first and basic act of theological work is prayer. . . . [It] is peculiar and characteristic of theology that it can be performed only in the act of prayer."[40] Theological work "must be that sort of act that has the manner and meaning of a prayer in all its dimensions, relationships, and movements."[41] Barth identifies four dimensions of the inseparable bond of prayer and theology.

1. Barth speaks first of the need for the theologian to turn away for a moment from his own efforts to the object of theology, the living God. "In prayer a man temporarily turns away from his own efforts. This move is necessary precisely for the sake of the duration and continuation of his own work."[42] Prayer is for theological work, Barth suggests, a kind of "Sabbath rest." This is not to say that prayer is a substitute for work. "A man prays, not in order to sacrifice his work or even to neglect it, but in order that it may not remain or become unfruitful work, so that he may do it under the illumination and, consequently, under the rule and blessing of God."[43]

2. Another dimension of the unity of prayer and theology identified by Barth is the fact that "the object of theological

work is not some thing but some one."[44] This means that "true and proper language concerning God will always be a response to God, which overtly or covertly, explicitly or implicitly, thinks and speaks of God exclusively in the second person. And this means that theological work must really and truly take place in the form of a liturgical act, as invocation of God, and as prayer."[45] Barth again cites the example of Anselm's *Proslogion*, which takes the form of a prayer from beginning to end. "Implicitly and explicitly, proper theology will have to be a *Proslogion*, *Suspirium*, or prayer."[46]

3. A third dimension of the relationship of prayer and theology for Barth is that theology can never build from past results with complete confidence but must always begin again from the beginning. Nothing should be allowed to harden, nothing taken as a matter of course from past theological work. Theological study must be permeated by the attitude of prayer if it is to be genuinely free to respond to the living word of God. "Every act of theological work must have the character of an offering in which everything is placed before the living God."[47] "Because it has to be ever renewed, ever original, ever ready to be judged by God himself and by God alone, theology must be an act of prayer."[48]

4. Finally, for Barth the work of theology presupposes that the object of this inquiry is the living and active God, who is self-revealing, and that the human beings who undertake the inquiry are capable of engaging in this work. On both counts, however, only God acting in free grace is able to satisfy these conditions. God alone can reveal God, and God alone can open our eyes and mind to the reality of God. Prayer thus belongs to theological work as a "double entreaty" for God's grace.[49] Theology must therefore proceed with the prayer "*Veni, Creator*

Spiritus!" "In his movements from below to above and from above to below, the one Holy Spirit achieves the opening of God for man and the opening of man for God. Theological work, therefore, lives by and in the petition for his coming."[50]

In this essay on prayer in *Evangelical Theology*, Barth gives his fullest description of prayer as a "habit" of theological work, a distinctive human attitude that is necessary in all theological inquiry. Without the attitude of prayer, theology quickly becomes captive to forces alien to its subject matter. As Barth describes the attitude of prayer in theological work, it is characterized by such traits as: persistent attentiveness to the object of inquiry rather than to the inquiring subject; faithful acknowledgment that this object is not at one's disposal, but a living personal subject who has spoken and acted in the past and who also continues to speak and act in new and surprising ways; humble readiness to eschew arrogance and defensiveness regarding the results of past inquiry and to begin anew at the beginning; viewing one's work as an offering to God to be purified, corrected, and used by God as God pleases; and joyful waiting on divine grace as a gift that must be received anew every day. Prayer and theological work go hand in hand whenever theology intends to be a genuinely free science.

Prayer, Divine Sovereignty, and Human Freedom

Throughout the *Church Dogmatics*, and particularly in his doctrine of providence, Barth addresses the persistent problem of the relationship of divine sovereignty and human freedom. He sees the underlying issue as not whether but in what way God is sovereign, and not whether but in what way the human creature is free. Controversy about these matters has often arisen, Barth thinks, because of misconceptions of divine sovereignty on the one hand and of the freedom of human beings as creatures on the other. According to Barth, misunderstandings about the relationship of divine sovereignty and human freedom stem from our anxiety that we may ascribe too much to God and too little to the creature. This anxiety has its root in the fact that we fear God more than we are able to love God.

> If our Christian perception and confession does not free us to love God more than we fear Him, then it is obvious that we shall necessarily fear Him more than we love Him. At root, this is the only relevant form of human sin. And this is the one and only reason it is so hard to grasp that the freedom of creaturely activity is confirmed by the unconditioned and irresistible lordship of God. And a reason of this kind cannot be disputed away by theological arguments. If we fear God and fear for ourselves, then we do fear. And since we, all of us, have the habit of fear of God, this habit will not go out of us except by prayer and fasting. All that we can say is that when and to the extent that it does really go out, the theological arguments which follow will acquire force and validity.[51]

This passage is noteworthy because it shows so clearly that, in Barth's view, successful theological work as faith's quest for greater understanding presupposes the attitude of prayer. He contends that the cogency of theological arguments does not depend solely on meeting formal criteria of truth such as the criteria of correspondence or coherence. Unless the attitude of prayer is present, unless

God is approached in prayer as sovereignly gracious, as the source of human freedom rather than a threat to it, as the object of our love and trust rather than our fear, then all attempts to resolve the debate about divine sovereignty and human freedom by argument, however strong or ingenious, are bound to be ineffective.

For Barth the God to whom we pray in the name of Jesus Christ is not the God depicted by what he calls the "miserable anthropomorphism" of divine immutability.[52] In contrast to Schleiermacher, who states that the "primary and basal presupposition" in his theology of prayer is that "there can be no relation of interaction between creature and Creator,"[53] Barth calls Christian theology to eschew "the hallucination of a divine immutability, which rules out the possibility that God can let Himself be conditioned in this or that way by His creature. God is certainly immutable. But He is immutable as the living God and in the mercy in which He espouses the cause of the creature. In distinction from the immovability of a supreme idol, His majesty, the glory of His omnipotence and sovereignty, consists in the fact that He can give to the requests of this creature a place in His will."[54] Just as the triune God is not alone in eternity, so God elects not to be alone in the divine activity ad extra. As the living God, God is free to converse with the creature, and "to allow himself to be determined by it in this relationship."[55]

Similarly, human beings are created and redeemed for communion with God and others. They are given a share in the lordship of God, and this happens supremely in the act of prayer. The God of sovereign grace "lets the creature, in its unity with Himself, participate in His omnipotence and work, in the magnifying of His glory and its own salvation, by commanding it to ask and hearing its requests, and when He truly gives it a place at His side in the kingdom of grace and the kingdom of the world. God cannot be greater than He is in Jesus Christ, the Mediator between Him and man. And in Jesus Christ He cannot be greater than He is when He lets those who are Christ's participate in His kingly office, and therefore when he not only hears but answers their requests."[56] God's sovereignty "is so great that it embraces both the possibility, and, as it is exercised, the actuality, that the creature can actively be present and co-operate in his overruling. There is no creaturely freedom that can limit or compete with the sole sovereignty and efficacy of God. But permitted by God, and indeed willed and created by Him, there is the freedom of the friends of God concerning whom He has determined that without abandoning the helm for one moment He will still allow Himself to be determined by them."[57]

In sum, God creates rather than crushes human freedom; God wills the "real co-operation" of human beings as covenant partners. Under the lordship of the God decisively made known in Jesus Christ, the human creature is not robbed of freedom or excluded from creative activity but is established as the friend of God, "a subject which in its own place and within its own limits has an actual voice and responsibility in the matter."[58] Genuine prayer is possible because the God of free grace wills to be vulnerable and wills the human creature to relate to God as a free subject and active partner of God.

For Barth, prayer is a correspondence in Christian life to the perfect co-presence in Jesus Christ of divine grace and human freedom without confusion or separation or loss of proper order. We may thus speak of Barth's understanding of prayer as involving a very special cooperation, a singular partnership, a "double agency," grounded in the person and work of the incarnate Lord. What George Hunsinger has called the Chalcedonian pattern in Barth's theology that "posits a relationship of asymmetry, intimacy, and integrity between God and the human being" reaches its highest point in Christian life in the act of prayer.[59]

The Freedom to Lament and Question God in Prayer

Barth's interpretation of the book of Job provides a test case of his understanding of prayer as an act of freedom, as centrally petition, and as a clue to the proper understanding of the relationship of divine sovereignty and human freedom. What can we say of Barth's analysis of prayer in face of Job's struggle with the mystery of evil and suffering?

Barth sharply contrasts the way the friends of Job relate to and speak of God with the way Job does. In a word, they speak defensively about God. They talk in abstractions and generalities; they utter timeless truths; their words are like "cut flowers."[60] Job, on the other hand, speaks out of the concrete history between God and him. Job does not have the luxury of looking over God's shoulder, as it were, or dispensing information about God. Job "simply stands before and under God."[61] He is engaged in an "eye-to-eye and mouth-to-ear encounter" with God.[62] Whereas for the friends of Job everything is fixed and predictable, for Job everything is open and in motion. He does not speak of God in well-worn phrases and old clichés. As God's living and free creature, Job addresses the living and free God. The anguish is that Job now experiences God as hidden and silent, and so he cries, argues, protests, and waits for God to speak and act again. Even in his complaint, confusion, and anger, Job thus speaks the truth in contrast to his friends, whose words are elegant and pious but false.

While the complaints and arguments of Job may not be classified as prayer according to strict definitions, they are certainly spoken in what Barth calls the attitude of prayer. However shocking, Job's witness to God is prayerful. Job knows that the deep hiddenness of God can be uncovered only by God. The truth of God must speak for itself. In the end, Job is brought to the truth that he seeks not by argument, but solely by God's own word and deed.

While his arresting exegesis of the book of Job provides impressive support of Barth's interpretation of prayer as the meeting place of divine and human freedom, the particular form Job's dialogue with God takes points to a certain deficiency in Barth's theology of prayer. More specifically, it raises questions as to whether Barth gives the prayer of lament its due as an essential form of biblical prayer. Does Barth tend to overlook or at least to subordinate the prayer of lament, protest, and anguished questioning?

For Barth, Job is a person who knows that God is free, and who has been freed by God. The free God and the freed human being are strange and incomprehensible to the defenders of God, who know only the "ignominious dependence and total unfreedom" of the *do ut des* relationship with God. Hence the friends of Job are "so very shocked by Job's obstinate protestation of his innocence, which in fact is nothing other than the freedom given him by God and exercised in relation to Him."[63] Barth clearly acknowledges the legitimacy of Job's lament and protest to God.

But does this formal acknowledgment work its way into Barth's theology of prayer? This question has at least three aspects: biblical, experiential, and christological.

1. As noted earlier, Barth defines prayer as centrally petition and sees all other forms of prayer—thanksgiving,

confession, adoration—in relation to this center. While there are some advantages to this centering of prayer, the hazards become especially evident in relation to the wide range of biblical prayers that include prayers of lament. Biblical laments are not adequately described as petition. If taken seriously, the psalms of lament, the laments of Jeremiah, Isaiah, and Job, and the cry of Jesus from the cross are prayers that question, protest, dare to remind God that things are not right, that redemption is not yet accomplished, that God's justice does not yet rule throughout the creation. In speaking of prayer as centrally petition, Barth tends toward a reductionism or at least toward a perilous systematization of the irreducible forms of prayer found in the biblical tradition. On numerous occasions, Barth himself underscores the dangers of a "systematic" impulse in theology; such dangers are apparent in his own theology of prayer.

2. Barth recognizes clearly that Job, in his experience of the hiddenness of God, cries, expresses outrage, even argues with God, and that God eventually declares that Job has spoken the truth in contrast to the self-appointed defenders of God. Job's experience is also the experience of countless believers. The problem is: Does Barth allow the distinctive prayer of lament and protest, etched in the biblical tradition and voiced by victims of injustice and abuse in every age, to deepen and enrich his overall theology of prayer? Is it not precisely this form of biblical prayer that is so disturbing, even stunning in contrast with conventional understandings and practices of prayer? Is not the depth of the dialogue between the God of the covenant and God's chosen covenant partner found precisely in the freedom of the covenant partner to challenge, question, even argue with God in the face of the power of evil and the still unrealized promises of

God? Does not prayer that fails to make room for lament and protest as an authentic form of prayer easily decline into the masquerade that Barth himself is eager to unmask?

An observation by Alan Torrance, a sympathetic inter-preter of Barth's work, is pertinent here:

> [Barth's] conception of Christian experience seems predominantly to be a joyful and optimistic one which is reflected perhaps in [his] at times almost embarrassingly extravagant praise and adulation of the music of Mozart. As a result, one feels compelled to ask whether this does not reflect the fact that, although Barth suffered family tragedy on more than one occasion, he did not seem to have to face guilt, or national shame, or the humiliation of his cause in the same way that, for example, a theologian like Jürgen Moltmann had to. As a result Moltmann seems to be able to express the Christian experience of God within the depths of guilt, of despair, of dis-illusionment and of hopelessness in a more pro-found and human way than Barth could have.[64]

What Torrance detects as missing in Barth's conception of Christian experience manifests itself, I am suggesting, in his insufficient attention to the prayer of lament in the biblical witness.

3. In his christocentric interpretation of prayer, Barth emphasizes that Jesus Christ is the true subject of prayer, the great suppliant and petitioner. Correspondingly, Christian prayer is a participation in the prayer of Jesus Christ. Yet Barth tends to emphasize our prayer far more as a participation in the kingly office of Christ than as a participation in the priestly office of Christ.

What remains underdeveloped in Barth's christocentric theology of prayer is the significance of Jesus' cry of abandonment as christological authorization of the cry of pain and protest by all who suffer injustice, who are oppressed, abused, tortured. Included in Jesus' representative act is his cry and lamentation on our behalf. Jesus is our representative, our great high priest, not only as the one who bears the consequences of our sins but also as one who laments on our behalf before God. He is the one who "in the days of his flesh . . . offered up prayers and supplications, with loud cries and tears, to the one who was able to save him from death" (Heb. 5:7).

Surely there has been an imbalance in many Christian theologies of prayer, inasmuch as abundant attention has been given to Jesus' acceptance of the will of God in the Gethsemane prayer but so little, if anything, has been said about the terrifying cry from the cross, precisely for our understanding of the freedom of authentic prayer. While acknowledging the uniqueness of Jesus' cry of abandonment, in which all our human cries are gathered up and presented to God on our behalf, we should also recognize that Jesus' cry is echoed in the cries of all who are abused and afflicted. The prayer of lament safeguards the fact that our prayers are uttered in the shadow of the cross as well as in the Easter hope of the triumph of God's grace throughout the creation, and that consequently room must be made in our personal and corporate prayers for "the Friday voice of faith."[65] The freedom to pray includes the freedom to petition, to praise, to confess, and to intercede; it also includes the freedom to cry out and protest against the continuing presence of injustice, violence, and oppression in the world.

Karl Barth on the Lord's Prayer

DONALD K. McKIM

T he issue of the Christian life is a perennial one for all Christians. The questions throng: What is its goal, its "shape"? What activities should the life of faith in Christ call us toward, religiously and culturally?

Karl Barth turned his attention to these matters in the posthumously published volume of his *Church Dogmatics* titled *The Christian Life*.[1] This work comprises Barth's final lecture fragments, the last words he left in his *Church Dogmatics*.

The fragments here would have eventually completed *CD* IV/4 on the Doctrine of Reconciliation. In 1967 a section entitled "Baptism as the Foundation of the Christian Life" was published (with English translation in 1969). This was section 75 of chapter XVII of Volume IV. In the present book, we have sections 74, 76, 77, and 78. Yet even with this, according to the editors, we have less than half of *Church Dogmatics* IV/4. So Barth has left an "unfinished symphony." Yet significantly, his final writings address the most practical of issues for the Christian: the life of prayer and how this life of prayer may be lived. For here we have Barth's discussion of the Lord's Prayer (sections 76–78). Unfortunately it breaks off after the second petition,

"Thy kingdom come." But what we do have is rich. For Barth viewed the Lord's Prayer as the heart of the ethics of the Christian life.

The Significance of the Lord's Prayer

Barth's original aim in *CD* IV/4 was to consider, under the doctrine of reconciliation, the "ethics of reconciliation" by using the rubric of "faithfulness." Barth intended to say that the concept of faithfulness was the hub around which the whole Christian life revolved. In the first version of the conclusion to section 74, Barth said the term "faithfulness"

> brings out most precisely what is now before us, the situation of the covenant, indeed, the covenant of grace, between God and man and therefore the Christian grace, between God and man and therefore the Christian life as the will of God which man must obediently do. The reconciliation of the world with God enacted in Jesus Christ is for God's relationship to man and man's to him a once-for-all, decisive, and basic act of his faithfulness. (280)

Correlatively, Barth writes that "Faithfulness to the faithful God is the one total thing that is required of man as the Christian life" (285).

But Barth changed his mind. Instead of working with the theme of faithfulness, he decided to order his material on the ethics of reconciliation around the controlling concept of "calling upon God." For this, the Lord's Prayer is the masterful model. The command of God the Reconciler is found in Psalm 50:15: "Call upon me." The Christian life is to be lived in obedience to this command. "Invocation," Barth wrote now, is "the basic meaning of every divine command" and is "the basic meaning of all human obedience." For "what God permits man, what he expects, wills, and requires of him, is a life of calling upon him" (44). This meant for Barth that attention should center on the Lord's Prayer. It is the prayer prayed by Jesus Christ, "the representative of all men," and the prayer he ordered his disciples to pray after him. Quoting Tertullian (*De oratione* I.6), Barth says this prayer is a "breviary of the whole gospel." Quoting Calvin, Barth indicates that the invocation of God is the "chief exercise of faith" (*Institutes* III.20). The Lord's Prayer is to be the "center of this chapter of special ethics" with two other themes belonging to the life and teaching of the church to mark its circumference (44). These themes speak respectively to the foundation of the Christian life and its continual renewal. The themes are Baptism, which Barth saw as providing the "prologue" to the chapter, and the Lord's Supper (which he did not live to write) as the "epilogue." But the center of the Christian life is the invoking of God. And the Lord's Prayer is the model *par excellence* of what God permits and commands of us in prayer.

It is fascinating to read how Barth arrives at this basic stance as he considers, in section 74 on "Ethics as a Task of the Doctrine of Reconciliation," the issue of "The Gracious God as the Commanding God." Barth probed here at one of the most basic of all theological/ethical questions. As he put it: "What is the one thing in the midst of the truly and not just apparently many things that the gracious God commands man?" What is the "most relevant term," the "most appropriate concept" for expressing what God commands and demands of humanity and what we must do to obey God's command?

Barth's basic premise is that "the command of God is in all cases the command of Jesus Christ and therefore the law of the gospel, the form of grace" (36). But in this stimulating section we see Barth wrestling with a number of concepts, all of which initially appear as splendid candidates for the honor of summing up most succinctly what God commands and requires. Among the contenders: the general concept of "the Christian life," "freedom," "repentance," "faith," and "thanksgiving," as well as "faithfulness," to which he gives much attention and which, as mentioned above, was his original rubric (see 37–42).

But Barth decides that what is most needed here is "a word or concept that will express the fact that some human *action* is at issue in the obedience which the gracious God commands of man." So he uses the term "invocation." This is the general key for ordering the special ethics of the doctrine of reconciliation. "We are speaking," says Barth, "of the humble and resolute, the frightened and joyful *invocation* of the gracious God in gratitude, praise, and above all petition" (43). For this, the Lord's Prayer is at the center as the model prayer, showing us "that we should pray," "what we should pray and how we should pray."

Thus, Barth saw the Lord's Prayer as tremendously significant for the formation of the Christian life. It will show us the goal of our life of faith, the concerns that should be foremost in our minds, and the passions that should motivate us as we live as the people of God in the modern world.

Exposition of the Lord's Prayer

§76 *The Children and Their Father*

Barth deals with the first two petitions of the Lord's Prayer in three sections: "The Children and Their Father" (§76), "Zeal for the Honor of God" (§77), and

"The Struggle for Human Righteousness" (§78). In the first of these sections, Barth has three parts: "The Father," "The Children," and "Invocation."

In the first of these sections, with a series of striking paragraphs extending over several pages, Barth begins each with the exclamation: "Father!" The address to God in this way is vocative, and, says Barth, "the primal act of the freedom Christians are given, the primal form of the faithfulness with which they may correspond to his faithfulness" (51). Used as such by Christians, "Father" gives "the required precision, the appropriate fullness, and the authentic interpretation to a word that in itself is indefinite, empty, and ambivalent, namely, the word 'God'" (53). This incredibly rich form of address is much more, Barth says, than Schleiermacher's definition of God as the "source of the feeling of absolute dependence." That, he argues, is unsatisfactory because "the source might finally be a neuter, an original 'It' or 'Something'" (57). But what we really have to do with in the Christian faith is a God who is Father "over his household," who "provides and teaches," who is Lord, King, and Judge in his kingdom, and who is Creator (57).

Yet beyond all this, God the Father is the "dear" Father for Christians. For God is "Abba, Father" and the language is of precious intimacy. Barth points out that in the New Testament, "God is Father because and insofar as Jesus Christ is his Son and he is the Father of Jesus Christ." Because of this intimate connection, he says, "there is, as a rule, little need to lay special stress on the Father's love, goodness, grace, and so forth, since it contains within itself all that need be said about the character of the divine Creator and Father as the fount and origin of all good things" (60). "God the Father of our Lord Jesus Christ" parallels the phrase "the Father of mercies and God of all comfort" from the Old Testament and thus the conception of God as the Father is found in Psalm 103; 2 Samuel 7:14f.; Deuteronomy 32:6, Hosea 11:1; Isaiah 63:15–17; etc. (60).

In this regard, "the people of Christ," says Barth, "can only join the people of Israel (61). We, as Christians, dare to call God "Father" because of the example and command of Jesus. Barth cites the prayers where Jesus addressed God in this way and reflects that Jesus' command, "Pray then like this," is the imperative "which is the basis of the vocative 'Father' in the thought and speech of Christians and hence also of their knowledge of the nature and existence of this God, whom there can be no question of their denying or exchanging for some other god." Thus, "our freedom to call upon God as Father is grounded absolutely in the way in which Jesus Christ called upon him, and still does so, when he turns to him" (65).

In his section on "The Children" Barth points out that this side of the eschaton, only a "prophetic minority"— Christians—are permitted to address God in this way. The closeness presupposed and the intimacy of the term is ours only by grace. For, "as a fish can breathe only in water and not on dry land, so Christians can live only as they drink from the fresh spring of free grace which is not natural, which cannot be won, but in which it pleases the Father continually to love his people and to call them his children" (78). We address God, Barth points out, as "*our* Father," not in the singular but in the plural. God is not just "Father in general," but "*your* Father and *mine*, and therefore *our* Father: the Father of each individual who may invoke him thus." God is "the common Father of all who believe and of all who will come to believe him, so that they are all brothers and sisters as his children" (82).

The children of God who are "liberated for invocation of God as their Father exist in responsibility to him and therefore to his people and therefore to each of its many members" (83).

The third part of Barth's chapter deals with "Invocation." Here he picks up the theme of what it means to address God as "Our Father" by pointing out that, when Christians make this address, they also include in their thought, "all those with whom they do not live as yet in this union of knowledge and confession because Jesus Christ is still a stranger to them. They cannot cry it in separation from the overwhelming host of half-believers, heretics, the superstitious, the unbelievers all around them" (100). Barth warns against turning our status as "God's children" into a "private club with a sacred private end." He argues that Christians "would not be taking seriously their ministry as witnesses of the reconciliation of the world with God accomplished in Jesus Christ . . . if they were to regard exclusively as their own Father the one whom they may know as Father in Jesus Christ." For, "apart from and in spite of what they deserve, by Jesus Christ and through his Spirit they have been taken up into *his* invocation of God as *his* Father. They have been liberated and empowered to follow him and join with him as his brethren in calling upon God as their Father too." Barth continues:

> As they make use of their freely given freedom to do this, they necessarily have to accept and make the same movement as that in which he associated them with himself. As his "My Father" opened up to include them, so their "Our Father" must open up to include those to whom he, being sent by his Father into the world, has sent them as witnesses of his sending. (100)

The "Our Father," argues Barth, is a "bold anticipation of the invocation to which in Jesus Christ . . . not they alone but these others are also ordained. In their name, then, and not just their own, they will cry 'Our Father,' as the provisional representatives and vicars of the rest"; these who are "not yet liberated and empowered and willing to do it, although they will not finally fail to do it when the lordship of Jesus Christ over all creation is manifested, and with it the reconciliation of the world to God that has taken place in him" (101).

For Barth, calling upon God in prayer is not a "monologue" or some "self-help theory" by which we seek uplift and a "spiritual high" all by ourselves. Rather, when God's children invoke God as "our Father," they do so not in the sense of a "venture, a mere gesture, a shot in the dark, an experiment, or a gamble" (104). Rather, they do so, says Barth, with the full expectation that God hears and that they "have a part in the history in which God is their partner and they are his partners, in which they are liberated for this action and summoned to it, in which there is also given to them the promise of his corresponding action and therefore of his hearing" (104). Barth says that "the only prayer that can be unanswered is prayer that is uncertain of an answer, so that it is not calling upon the true God" (105). God hears our thanksgivings, and our petitions. Quoting Paul Gerhardt: "No little tear is too small before Him."

So in section 76, Barth strongly establishes the basis of prayer and explores what it means to pray, "Our Father."

§77 *Zeal for the Honor of God*

Barth's exposition catches fire in §77. He begins with the statement: "Christians are people with a definite passion.

In no circumstances, then, can they be cowards, blind-worms, bored, boring, or commonplace" (111). What is the distinctive Christian passion? It is "concern for the honor of God. This is at issue in the first petition: God's hallowing of his name" (113). A better term than "desire for the honor of God" is "zeal for the honor of God," says Barth. "Zeal" clearly speaks of a passion and has "a predominantly positive sense in both the Old Testament and the New Testament." And Barth questions if there has ever been a "great Christian who has not in his own way had a fiery zeal for God" (115).

In his discussion of "the Known and Unknown God," Barth speaks of "three concentric circles in which God is known and unknown in different ways, in which his name is hallowed and honored as it should be, but also desecrated, disputed, and slandered" (116). The world is the outer circle; the church (as a theological community) is the middle circle and the inner and outer personal life of the Christian is the inner circle. These all overlap and do not simply coincide. In these three realms we live with the *simul*, the "and at the same time." We "know" God, and yet "at the same time" God is "unknown" in the world, in the church, and in ourselves.

When God commands us to pray, "Hallowed be Thy Name," says Barth, we are not merely expressing some "wish of human longing . . . that in the course of an historical process which is perhaps already in motion it will somehow come about that the sanctification of the name of God will go ahead in the world, the church, and Christians" (159). Rather, the work of hallowing God's name is a work of God himself. When Christians invoke God for this, they are coming from Good Friday and Easter Day and they are praying for "the taking place of the unique and definitive divine act" which they know has "taken place already in Jesus Christ" (163). We can make this petition, says Barth, "only as we come from the one in whom it is already fulfilled" (167). This glorifying of the name of God was done once in Jesus Christ and it will be done again as well. The petition has an eschatological dimension. For there will come a day, indeed the "last day" when the dialectic of the "already" and "not yet" of the kingdom of God will be overcome finally. Then the Victor, Jesus Christ, who is seen as victor now to those who know him by faith, will be "seen and looked upon and touched by all and in all (1 John 1:1) as he was by his first disciples at the commencement of his *parousia* on Easter Day" (168).

What does the praying of these petitions mean for Christians? What does it mean that we have "zeal for the honor of God" and pray that God's name might be hallowed? For Barth this means the "Precedence of the Word of God." He concludes §77 with a discussion of the thesis that "the law of prayer is the law of action" (168) and that in our being commanded to pray for these things, the practical result for us is that "those who look back to the first revelation of the hallowing of God's name that took place in Jesus Christ, and who also look forward to its second and final revelation, cannot come to terms and be satisfied with the status quo" (173). This is the springboard for Christian action, indeed for "revolt," says Barth. We who pray for the "future sanctifying of God's name cannot accept its present desecration." So we are in "revolt and resistance against the regime of vacillation" (174). In all we do as Christians, precedence over every other factor must be given to the Word of God which we have heard and which we will hear again in Jesus Christ. Again Barth uses the figure of the three circles: the world, the church, and the individual life, to say that in all, we must "swim against the tide" (194) if need be, to be obedient first and foremost to that Word of God in Jesus Christ. All Christian action, all Christian motivation for action is grounded, finally in our "zeal for the honor of God."

§78 The Struggle for Human Righteousness

The second petition of the Lord's Prayer is "Thy Kingdom Come." In §78 Barth writes on this under the theme "The Struggle for Human Righteousness." In these last pages, we find some of Barth's keenest insights.

"The genuineness of human zeal for God's honor needs testing." That's how Barth begins, and he does not end until he has filled out fully the ways in which our testings take place.

We are first in a "Revolt against Disorder." "Zeal for God's honor can be good, obedient, and full of promise," writes Barth, "only when it is directly accompanied by the struggle for human righteousness" (206). The *militia Christi* imagery of the Christian life as warfare is picked up here with Barth's comment that "Christians are summoned by God's command not only to zeal for God's honor but also to a simultaneous and related revolt, and therefore to entry into a conflict." For Christians always exist under "a binding requirement to engage in a specific uprising" (207).

There are numerous kinds of revolts in which Christians as persons may be engaged. They may be in conflict for their freedom, for example, against all enemies and restrictors of that freedom: against the painful conditions of life, against unwanted destinies, or supremely against "tyrants, those by whom they find themselves browbeaten, defrauded, and oppressed" (207). Yet this is not the Christian's true revolt. Rather "the general plight against which Christians are commanded to revolt and fight is the disorder which both inwardly and outwardly controls and penetrates and poisons and disrupts all human relations and interconnections (211). This disorder arises from and consists in "deviation from order." The human race, says Barth, "exists in such deviation. The order from which it deviates is the form of an obedient life of people in fellowship with God which includes as such the corresponding form—the guarantee of human right, freedom, and peace—of a life of people in fellowship with one another" (211). This is the decisive action into which our calling upon God in the second petition of the Lord's Prayer, "thy kingdom come," leads us. God's kingdom comes from God. It is not ours to win by human effort. The kingdom is, writes Barth,

> the universal and definitive revelation of the righteousness of God which judges and establishes humanity. It is the institution of his perfect lordship in human relations and interconnections. It is the setting up of his salutary order in human life and fellowship. The kingdom of God is God himself in the act of normalizing human existence. It is thus God himself in the victorious act of overcoming the disorder which still rules humanity. (212)

"Christians have the freedom," says Barth, "to pray that God's kingdom, God himself in this act, will appear and come—will come to us from heaven to earth."

In his subsection on "The Lordless Powers," Barth describes the manner and nature of the evil which Christians call upon God to set aside in this second petition.

Ultimately the root of this evil disorder that God's kingdom overcomes is human sin. Alienation from God is the source of self-alienation and alienation of humans from each other (213). When humans try to live a "lord-less life," various forms of disorder appear. These disorders are powers, which themselves are "lordless" as the New Testament witness abundantly asserts (217). These "powers" are limited by Jesus Christ, who is far above these forces (Eph. 1:21), who has "triumphed over them at the very point where they seemed to triumph over him, namely, in his crucifixion (Col. 2:14)," and who will finally be ultimately destroyed at his *parousia* (1 Cor. 15:24). Yet these powers are still real and potent in the here and now.

One of Barth's most fascinating discussions is his analysis of these "lordless powers" which the authors of the New Testament refrain from naming specifically or describing, "possibly," Barth says, "because they could assume that they were already clear enough to their readers" (219). In this section Barth discusses political absolutisms (219) and "the demonic which is visibly at work in *all* politics" (emphasis added); mammon, the love of money (222ff.); ideologies, in which even the so-called "human ideal" can become an idol, and of which "slogans or catchwords" are propaganda signs (224ff.). These are spiritual forces which as "lordless powers" are now engaged in warfare against God.

There is a second general group of such forces and these are *chthonic* forces. These are the lordless powers of the earth that rob us of our freedom "under the pretext and appearance of granting every kind of freedom" (229). These include such powers as technology, under which Barth touches on such items as fashions in clothing and "sport." He asks: "What is behind the enthusiasm of millions of sporting fans who watch the players with such passionate and often frenzied excitement? What has made the industrializing and commercializing of sport so clearly remunerative?" (229).

Barth goes on here to cite the example of the soccer championship games in Sweden in 1958 which Brazil won. They were led by the prodigy Péle, then only seventeen years old. What earth-force is it, asks Barth, that led Péle to be offered such large sums of money "and many other good things," and also to receive "no fewer than five hundred offers of marriage, while on the same occasion Germany, for the opposite reason, threatened to plunge into a kind of irritated national mourning with all kinds of accompanying phenomena? Why all this fuss and fury?" (230).

Even transportation and all the hustle and bustle of human life comes under Barth's scrutiny. He asks: "Has life really become easier and not harder through our happily achieved accelerations? Or are we expecting that all this will come with increased speed, with the help of atomically propelled vehicles or the development of cosmic carriages when the moon itself will not be worth looking at by those who are on the way to Venus?" (231). But all these powers, all these forces, can disrupt life and cause people to become "people of disorder" (233). They can tear the individual apart, and, "because there are so many of them and in such competition—they tear apart society also." But "over against the kingdom of human disorders stands the kingdom of the divine order" (233).

It is for this kingdom that we have the freedom to call upon God when we pray, "Thy Kingdom Come." In this his third subsection, Barth deals with the meaning of this, even though he admits that "the Kingdom of God defies expression" (237) for it is ultimately a "mystery" (239).

Barth devotes several pages of small type here to outlining a history of views about the kingdom of God

(240–244). But from the New Testament, Barth says, we see two things: first, the kingdom has a "strictly eschatological content and character, that is, that it looks toward an act of God as the goal and end of all human history"; and second, the kingdom has "its basis and meaning in the totality of this history," in a "definite event within it" (247). What *is* the kingdom of God? What is its center, the event in history on which it is based? Barth answers simply: Jesus Christ. It is *his* history, indeed his person which is the kingdom of God in our midst. Barth agrees with Tertullian (and we might add Origen as well) when Tertullian wrote: "In the gospel Christ Himself is the kingdom of God" (252 citing *Adv. Marc.*, IV. xxxii, 8; 252). The kingdom is *autobasileia*, a self-kingdom. The Kingdom is a "he," not an "it," and in Jesus Christ both future expectation and present fulfillment are realized (254). By the Holy Spirit we recollect history past and we anticipate history future, as the Kingdom of God in Jesus Christ becomes real to us now in the present by the power of God which is the Holy Spirit. To end it all, Barth cites the saying of the Blumhardts: "Jesus is Victor."

The final subsection, which ends *The Christian Life*, is Barth's discussion *Fiat Iustitia*, on the doing of righteousness (260ff.). When we pray, "Thy kingdom come," says Barth, we are commanded to pray this petition "bravely" (262) and we are summoned ourselves at the same time, to use our freedom to live "with a view to the coming kingdom" of God (263). We are not permitted as Christians, Barth writes, to live in light of the resurrection of Christ, anticipating the dawning of the day of God's final righteousness in him by being idle now, acquiescing in human unrighteousness and disorder and all its consequences. We may not live now "in the mortal imperiling of life, freedom, peace, and joy on earth under the lord-

ship of the lordless powers" and with the "gloomy skeptical speculation to find comfort in the thought that until
God's final and decisive intervention, the course of events
will necessarily be not only as bad as previously but
increasingly worse" (263). No, says Barth, Christians are
to wait and hasten toward the dawn of God's day. "They
wait by hastening," he says. For

> their waiting takes place in the hastening. Aiming at
> God's kingdom, established on its coming and not
> on the status quo, they do not just look toward it but
> run toward it as fast as their feet will carry them.
> This is inevitable if in their hearts and on their lips
> the petition "Thy kingdom come" is not an indolent
> and despondent prayer but one that is zealous and
> brave. (263)

To pray this second petition, "Thy kingdom come,"
asserts Barth, is to say, "Christians are claimed for action
in the effort and struggle for human righteousness" (264).
We know full well that God's righteousness is "God's own
act, which has already been accomplished and is still
awaited" in Jesus Christ. But now, in the "time between
that beginning and that end, our time as the time of the
presence of Jesus Christ in the Holy Spirit, is for Christians the space for gratitude, hope, and prayer, and also
the time of responsibility for the occurrence of human
righteousness" (264).

What is this "human righteousness" in which we are to
be involved as Christians? Barth says the speech and
action of Christians must "in all circumstances take place
with a view to people, in address to people, and with the
aim of helping people" (266). The object of our thought,
speech, and action must be other humans. For God himself

willed to become a human; Jesus Christ lived, died, and rose again for humanity; and Jesus Christ promised his Holy Spirit to human beings. "We are not our own but God's," says Calvin (*Institutes* III.7.1). "We do not belong to ourselves but to the Lord," says Barth, "but because the Lord is the Father, Son, and Holy Spirit who bound and obligated himself to man, Christians also belong to mankind and in this concrete sense they belong to themselves" (267). As Christians we are not exempt from our own shares in the evil and corruption of this world. But we have been "required and empowered to pray for the coming of the kingdom." We are to swim against the stream "regardless of the cost or consequences." We do this by "looking past and beyond all other things" to the human beings whom God has loved in spite of all their corruption and misery. And we make the human "right and life and freedom and joy" our theme.

So we are from the start humanists. Our concern is for the other, the one for whom Jesus Christ came, lived, and died. The Christian does not see the clothes that are worn—"Sunday clothes or working clothes or fool's clothes." The Christian does not see the other as political or economic or ecclesiastical, as "a member of this or that country or sociological stratum, nor as the type of this or that psychological category, nor as one who believes in this or that doctrine of salvation or perdition." Christians will not see the other as "a good citizen or a convict, as the representative of a conviction or party that they find agreeable or painful, as a Christian or non-Christian, as a good or bad, a practicing or non-practicing Christian." These are "garbs or masks" that are worn. Beneath them, we see the one before us as one whom God loves; one who is in need of grace. To that person, we offer the hope of the Christian gospel. This is the missionary task. While we practice it, we also practice the "little righteousness" which is our portion, "in contrast and yet also in correspondence with the great righteousness that God has practiced, practices, and will still practice" (270). In this "time between the times" we offer to the other standing before us the word of promise: that God has not abandoned you; that he will not do so; and that God's kingdom, "the kingdom of the Father, Son, and Holy Spirit, has come and will come," even for you; that "Jesus Christ is your hope" (271).

Concluding Reflections

Karl Barth gave a fitting capstone to his *Church Dogmatics*, though his ultimate goals were left unreached. His descriptions of the shape and contours of the Christian life will be most helpful for those who make the effort to understand the lineaments of Barth's thought. He addresses essential questions and his probing mind, his exegesis of Scripture, and his desire to proclaim Jesus Christ in the midst of the modern world can only be gratefully greeted by contemporary Christians.

Theologians will be hard at work in detecting shifts in emphasis or nuances between this final work and Barth's other writings. One has asked whether in this volume Barth has taken "adequate account of the covenantal relation between God and people.'"[2] He points out that "Barth made much of the covenant in earlier volumes, but in this one it is barely mentioned, and the relation between God and people is poised on an unstructured grace, which robs the Christian life of that confidence and peace and rest, which are attributed to it in the New Testament."[3]

A better appraisal would be that the covenant of grace is constantly presupposed throughout this book, especially in light of Barth's comments that in the covenant of grace God and humanity are "partners who are inseparably bound to one another" (28) and that in the covenant "God himself, in spite of everything that might argue against it, constantly unites and commits and pledges himself to be man's God, to be his wisdom, righteousness, sanctification, and redemption" (1 Cor. 1:30; [39]; cf. 64, 74).

Yet beside the verdicts of the scholars of Barth will stand the contributions of this book to the life of the wider church and to our understandings of the Christian life itself. Barth gives us a magnificent view.[4] Three points following the three major divisions of Barth's treatment of the Lord's Prayer suggest themselves.

1. Barth shows us the *confidence of the Christian life*. Jesus Christ is the fulfillment of the covenant of grace, and in him we gain the freedom to address God in terms of the most precious intimacy (65). This gives the Christian life the strongest note of confidence and hope. Thanksgiving, praise, and petition from the children of God are all heard by the God the Father. Barth goes so far as to say that "no request by any child of God is not fulfilled by God his Father" (107). There are no "unanswered prayers"! God may correct or transform our petitions. But for believers, "in all circumstances they can be sure of an answer. In all circumstances it will come to them in the form determined by their Father" (108). This is possible because we pray not in our own names, but in the name of God's Son, Jesus Christ. For in him we have access to the Father (John 14:13f.; 16:23f.; [108]). This assurance is the source of the strongest confidence for facing life: We are heard and cared for by our heavenly Father.

2. Barth also pinpoints the *motivation of the Christian life*. He names it "zeal for the honor of God" and calls it the Christian's "great passion." If "the law of prayer is the

law of action" (168), then prayer for the "hallowing of God's name" takes on the most potent significance. What greater impetus or keener incentive can there be than the desire for the name of God and the Word of God to take precedence in all the arenas of life? Barth believed this is an attainable possibility for the people of God. He wrote: "To allow and give the Word of God the precedence over other constitutive factors in their lives—that is something that can take place. It *can* be done" (178). Barth was under no illusion that this was possible fully, this side of the eschaton. He warned that a believer "should not try to be a Christian Hercules." For we "can neither repeat nor anticipate God's victory" in Jesus Christ (181). Barth would rule out activism for the sake of activism alone. The Christian is "a child and citizen of the world" (194). In this world the Christian is impelled and propelled by this zeal for the honor of God. No sphere or arena of life is exempt from the Christian's passion to be a "witness" to the Word (201) and to bring the Word of God—Jesus Christ—to bear on the full range of human ideas and endeavors.

3. Barth further sets before us the *task of the Christian life*. This he describes as "the struggle for human right-eousness" in view of the petition, "Thy kingdom come." He urges "struggle" and "revolt" against all the disorders of the human condition and human "unrighteousness" (211). Yet Barth keeps things in biblical perspective. His prescriptions make it clear that in the struggles against the "Lordless powers" which demonically seek their way with this world, the Christian has an ultimate allegiance. This is to Jesus Christ and to his kingdom. With this view, Christians must never absolutize the causes to which they give themselves. They must never completely identify the revolts, revolutions, and struggles—in which they may legitimately take part—with the ultimate task, goal, and

Notes

Hesselink: Karl Barth on Prayer

1. *Prayer: According to the Catechisms of the Reformation*, trans. Sara F. Terrien (Philadelphia: Westminster Press, 1952, 2nd ed., 1985, ed. Don E. Saliers). This is based on three seminars Barth held in Neuchâtel between 1947 and 1949 [reprinted above.].

2. G. C. Berkouwer, *The Triumph of Grace in the Theology of Karl Barth* (Grand Rapids: Eerdmans, 1956).

3. Hans Urs von Balthasar, *The Theology of Karl Barth* (San Francisco: Ignatius Press, 1992. The original German version was published in 1951. There was also an earlier English version.)

4. Herbert Hartwell, *The Theology of Karl Barth. An Introduction* (London: Duckworth, 1964).

5. *Church Dogmatics* [hereafter *CD*] III/3, *The Doctrine of Creation*, trans. Geoffrey W. Bromiley (Edinburgh: T. & T. Clark, 1961; original German edition appeared in 1950), 264–88.

6. *CD* III/4, *The Doctrine of Creation*, trans. Geoffrey W. Bromiley (Edinburgh: T. & T. Clark, 1961; original German edition, 1951), 87–115.

7. Karl Barth, *Evangelical Theology: An Introduction*, trans. Grover Foley (New York: Holt, Rinehart & Winston, 1963).

8. *The Christian Life: Church Dogmatics, Volume IV, Part 4: Lecture Fragments*, trans. Geoffrey W. Bromiley (Grand Rapids: Eerdmans, 1981; original German edition, 1976).

9. Cf. the essay by Lou Shapiro, "Karl Barth's Understanding of Prayer," *Crux* 24, 1 (March 1988), 26–33; the earlier piece by

Donald K. McKim, "Karl Barth on the Lord's Prayer" in *The Center Journal* 2, 1 (winter 1982) [reprinted below]; the frequent references to Barth's doctrine of prayer in Donald G. Bloesch, *The Struggle of Prayer* (San Francisco: Harper & Row, 1980), and Jan Milic Lochman, *The Lord's Prayer* (Grand Rapids: Eerdmans, 1990); and the brief notice in George Hunsinger's two books on Barth: *How to Read Karl Barth: The Shape of His Theology* (New York: Oxford University Press, 1991); *and Disruptive Grace: Studies in the Theology of Karl Barth* (Grand Rapids: Eerdmans, 2000).

10. *The Göttingen Dogmatics: Instruction in the Christian Religion*, trans. Geoffrey W. Bromiley, vol. 1 (Grand Rapids: Eerdmans, 1991), 3. Barth began these lectures in 1924.

11. Ibid., 3–4.

12. *Evangelical Theology*, 159.

13. Ibid., 160.

14. Ibid. Barth is fond of this Franciscan maxim and cites it in other contexts. See, e.g., *CD* III/4, 534.

15. Karl Barth, *Ethics*, ed. Dietrich Braun, trans. Geoffrey W. Bromiley (New York: Seabury Press, 1981).

16. The editor of *Ethics*, Dietrich Braun, sees in these lectures the basis for Barth's later treatment of ethics in the *Church Dogmatics*, despite various modifications.

17. At the end of his Prolegomena, *CD* I/2, Barth also has a chapter on ethics. Cf. his discussion of general ethics in II/2.

18. *Church Dogmatics* IV/4, *The Doctrine of Reconciliation: Fragment*, trans. Geoffrey W. Bromiley (Edinburgh: T. & T. Clark, 1969). The treatment here (on baptism) is already 213 pages.

19. *CD* III/4, 89.

20. Ibid., 92.

21. *The Christian Life*, xi, 44.

22. Ibid., 63. "The God who rules thus in Jesus Christ, the gracious God, is the God who commands" (ibid., 16). "The freedom of the children of God to do what they are commanded to do is purely and simply the work and gift of grace that is addressed to them and recognized by them" (ibid., 71).

23. *CD* III/3, 268.

24. *The Christian Life*, 44. This text is cited only in passing in *CD* III/4, 93, 95 and not at all in the discussion of prayer in III/3.

25. Ibid., 85.
26. This, in effect is the criticism of Lou Shapiro, who feels that "Barth's assertion that all prayer is petitionary is too strong." *Crux* 24, 1 (March 1988): 31.
27. Cf. *Prayer*, 38ff.; 2d ed., 47ff. [26ff.]; *CD* III/3, 270f., 284ff.; *CD* III/4, 88f.; and above all, *The Christian Life*, which treats only the first two petitions of the Lord's Prayer.
28. *CD* III/3, 270.
29. *CD* III/4, 87. Cf. p. 99 where Barth discusses thanksgiving, penitence, and worship as elements of prayer.
30. *The Christian Life*, 53. Barth also points out that in the Psalms a common theme is thanksgiving and praise, the latter "being simply an enhanced form of thanksgiving" (ibid., 87).
31. Ibid., 86.
32. *CD* III/3, 284.
33. *The Christian Life*, 103. Barth is thinking here of Schleiermacher and others who understand prayer as "the supreme and most intimate act of self-help" (ibid.).
34. See the winter issue of the *Reformed Review* 53, 2 (1999–2000). The theme is "What Happens When We Pray?" There are three responses to psychologist David Myers's essay, "Is Prayer Clinically Effective?" Myers's answer is negative, although he believes prayer has many benefits. The response by Leanne Van Dyk is more positive about the efficacy of petitionary prayer and takes an approach similar to Barth. See pp. 115–16.
35. Ibid., 102. What Myers is rightly reacting against is the notion that by prayer we can manipulate or coerce God into responding to our desires.
36. *CD* III/4, 96.
37. Cited first in *CD* III/4, 93, along with texts like Ps. 50:15; Jer. 29:12 and 33:3; Phil. 4:6; and Jude 20f.
38. *The Christian Life*, 104.
39. Ibid., 107. "The Christian asks, and by this asking the doors are opened wide, and the gates are lifted up, that the King of glory may come in" (*CD* III/3, 274).
40. Ibid., 105.
41. Ibid. We must be humble in prayer for we are unworthy supplicants, but at the same time our requests can be "frank, free, glad and bold" (*CD* III/4, 102).
42. *CD* III/3, 252-53, 270.

43. Ibid., 106–7, *CD* III/4, 106–107; *CD* III/3, 270.

44. *CD* III/3, 270.

45. Ibid., 271.

46. *CD* IV/1, 315.

47. *CD* III/3, 274. This point requires further elaboration, for here Barth indulges in some peculiarly Barthian logic that is not easy to follow. One further quote must suffice: "As the Son of God, he was the divine gift and answer, but as the Son of Man he was human asking. In him, God interceded for the creature. . . . And in him, the creature entered into the right and profitable relationship to God" (ibid., 274–75).

48. *CD* III/4, 94. "We may think of the intervention of Jesus Christ and the Holy Spirit which makes our human asking a movement in the cycle which goes out from God and returns to God. This means that although what we do is in itself very unholy, even when we pray, it will not fail to be sanctified" (*CD* III/4, 101).

49. *CD* III/3, 283.

50. Ibid., 264-65.

51. *The Christian Life*, 106.

52. Ibid.

53. Ibid., 107–8.

54. Process theologians such as Charles Hartshorne and John Cobb pay little attention to Barth, but the feminist theologian Sheila Greeve Davaney in her book *Divine Power* (Philadelphia: Fortress Press, 1986) contrasts the views of Barth and Hartshorne and opts for the latter. Donna Bowman, *The Divine Decision: A Process Doctrine of Election* (Louisville, Ky.: Westminster John Knox Press, 2002) focuses on Barth's doctrine of election in relation to Process thought. Cf. the critique of Barth in Langdon Gilkey, *Reaping the Whirlwind: A Christian Interpretation of History* (New York: Seabury Press, 1976). The issue has been raised afresh by the evangelical neo-Arminians (my term), the "open theists" or "openness of God" theologians who are challenging the traditional Augustinan-Reformed view of providence and prayer, including that of Barth. See John Sanders, *The God Who Risks: A Theology of Providence* (Downers Grove, Ill.: InterVarsity Press, 1998).

55. *Prayer*, 21; 2d ed. 33 [13].

56 *The Christian Life*, 106.

57. *Prayer*, 29; 2d ed. 41 [20].

58. *The Christian Life*, 105. Cf. *CD* III/3.

59. *Ibid.*, 104.

60. *CD* III/3, 286.

61. Ibid., 285.

62. *Prayer*, 22-23; 2d ed. 35 [14].

63. *CD* III/3, 285.

64. Ibid., 288.

65. *The Christian Life*, 102.

66. Ibid., 105.

67. Ibid., 105–6.

68. Ibid., 103–4.

69. George Hunsinger, *How to Read Karl Barth* (New York: Oxford University Press, 1991), 222. The conception of double agency "posits a relationship of asymmetry, intimacy, and integrity between God and the human being. It posits a fellowship of mutual coinherence and mutual self-giving, mediated in and by Jesus Christ" (ibid., 223). I would add, "and through the power of the Holy Spirit."

70. Ibid., 223–24.

71. *CD* III/4, 91ff. Calvin, in his brief but magisterial treatment of prayer in the *Institutes* III.20, gives four "rules" (*lex*) of prayer.

72. *CD* III/4, 91.

73. Ibid., 93.

74. Ibid., 97.

75. Ibid., 101. In this connection, Barth appears to approve of the prayer of an American general during World War II who prayed for deliverance "from this untimely rain" during the Ardennes offensive of 1944.

76. Ibid., 102f.

77. Ibid., 106.

78. Ibid., 107.

79. Ibid., 110-11.

80. Ibid., 111.

81. Ibid., 111-12.

82. Ibid., 112.

83. Ibid.

84. Ibid., 113.

85. Ibid., 113-14.

86. Ibid., 115.
87. Ibid., 114–15.
88. *Prayer: According to the Catechisms of the Reformation.* The first American edition was published by Westminster Press in 1952. A second edition edited by Don E. Saliers was published in 1985, again by Westminster Press. The translation is only slightly modernized, but there is a new introductory essay, "Prayer and Theology in Karl Barth" by Saliers, and in this edition there is a selection of Barth's pastoral prayers. [This edition is presented above.]
89. *CD* III/3, 268.
90. *The Christian Life*, 50. For some inexplicable reason Barth does not cite the original version of this adage: "lex orandi lex credendi."
91. *CD* III/4, 112.
92. *Prayer*, 22; 2d ed. 35 [14]; *The Christian Life*, 105. This phrase comes from Calvin's Geneva Catechism, Q. 252. Calvin then adds, ". . . since he gives us entrance and audience, and intercedes for us (Rom. 8:34)."
93. *CD* III/4, 103.
94. Ibid., 104. God "does not wish to act, exist, live, labor, work, strive, vanquish, reign and triumph without the human race. God does not wish, then, for his cause to be his alone; he wishes it to be ours as well" (*Prayer*, 38; 2d ed. 48 [27]).
95. "Jesus Christ is the donor and the warrant of the divine Fatherhood and of our filiality." *Prayer*, 36; 2d ed. 45 [24].
96. *CD* III/4, 105.
97. *Prayer*, 41; 2d ed. 51 [30].
98. Ibid., 55; 2d ed. 65 [43].
99. Ibid., 57; 2d ed. 66 [44].
100. In addition to the comprehensive but brief treatment of the Lord's Prayer in *Prayer*, cf. Donald McKim's fine summary and analysis of Barth's discussion of the first two petitions in *The Christian Life* in "Karl Barth on the Lord's Prayer" [below].
101. *Prayer*. 2d ed., 19–20 [xix–xx].
102. *Deliverance to the Captives* (London: SCM Press, 1961). A separate selection of Barth's prayers (in German) has also been published in a lovely little booklet, *Gebete*, with a foreword by Barth (Munich: Chr. Kaiser Verlag, 1964).
103. *Prayer*. 2d ed., 89 [67].

Migliore: Freedom to Pray

1. See Gustavo Gutiérrez, *We Drink from Our Own Wells: The Spiritual Journey of a People* (Maryknoll, N.Y.: Orbis Books, 1984).
2. Karl Barth, *Evangelical Theology*, trans. Grover Foley (Garden City, N.Y.: Doubleday & Co., Anchor Books, 1964), xi. Hereafter *ET*.
3. Karl Barth, *Church Dogmatics* III/4, trans. A. T. Mackay et al. (Edinburgh: T. & T. Clark, 1961), 91–92. Hereafter volumes of the *Church Dogmatics* will be cited by *CD* followed by volume and part number.
4. *CD* III/4, 92.
5. *CD* III/3, 269.
6. Ibid., 270.
7. Ibid., 269.
8. Ibid., 267–68.
9. Friedrich Schleiermacher, *The Christian Faith*, ed. H. R. Mackintosh and J. S. Stewart (Edinburgh: T. & T. Clark, 1928), 671.
10. *CD* III/4, 97.
11. *CD* III/3, 268.
12. *CD* III/4, 98.
13. Ibid.
14. Ibid.
15. Karl Barth, *The Christian Life: Church Dogmatics IV/4: Lecture Fragments*, trans. Geoffrey W. Bromiley (Grand Rapids: Eerdmans, 1981), 43.
16. *CD* III/3, 280.
17. *CD* III/4, 274–75.
18. *CD* III/3, 275.
19. Ibid., 276.
20. Ibid., 277.
21. Ibid., 282.
22. *CD* III/4, 108.
23. *CD* III/3, 283.
24. Ibid.
25. Ibid.
26. *CD* III/4, 110.
27. Ibid., 279.
28. Ibid., 280.
29. Ibid., 264.

30. *CD* IV/3.2, 882.
31. Ibid.
32. Ibid., 883.
33. *CD* III/4, 97.
34. Ibid., 111.
35. Ibid.
36. *CD* I/1, 23.
37. Ibid.
38. Ibid.
39. Ibid., 24.
40. *ET*, 141.
41. Ibid.
42. Ibid., 143.
43. Ibid., 144.
44. Ibid.
45. Ibid., 145.
46. Ibid.
47. Ibid., 147.
48. Ibid., 147.
49. Ibid., 149.
50. Ibid., 150.
51. *CD* III/3, 147–48.
52. *CD* III/4, 108.
53. Schleiermacher, *The Christian Faith*, 673.
54. *CD* III/4, 109.
55. *CD* III/3, 285.
56. *CD* III/4, 109.
57. *CD* III/3, 285.
58. Ibid., 286.
59. George Hunsinger, *How to Read Karl Barth: The Shape of His Theology* (New York: Oxford University Press, 1991), 221–24.
60. *CD* IV/3.1, 457.
61. Ibid.
62. Ibid., 458.
63. Ibid., 461.
64. Alan Torrance, "Christian Experience and Divine Revelation in the Theologies of Friedrich Schleiermacher and Karl Barth," in *Christian Experience in Theology and Life*, ed. I. Howard Marshall (Edinburgh: Rutherford House Books, 1988), 111.

65. Walter Brueggemann, "The Friday Voice of Faith," *Reformed Worship* 30 (December 1993): 2–5.

McKim: Karl Barth on the Lord's Prayer

1. Karl Barth, *The Christian Life: Church Dogmatics, Volume IV, Part 4: Lecture Fragments*, trans. Geoffrey W. Bromiley (Grand Rapids: Eerdmans, 1981). All further page references in this text will be to this volume.
2. George S. Hendry, "The Christian Life: *Church Dogmatics* IV/4, Lecture Fragments," *Theology Today* (April 1982): 75.
3. Ibid., 75.
4. Hendry seems to suggest that Barth "may have created the Christian in his own image" (75).

Contributors

I. John Hesselink is Professor of Systematic Theology Emeritus at Western Theological Seminary, Holland, Michigan.

Donald K. McKim is Academic and Reference Editor for Westminster John Knox Press.

Daniel L. Migliore is Charles Hodge Professor of Systematic Theology at Princeton Theological Seminary.

Don E. Saliers is Franklin Nutting Parker Professor of Theology and Worship at Candler School of Theology, Emory University.

I. John Hesselink's essay was originally presented for the conference "Karl Barth: Theology for Preaching and Prayer," on March 16, 2001, in Holland, Michigan.

Donald K. McKim's essay originally appeared in *The Center Journal* 2, 1 (winter 1982): 81–99.

Daniel L. Migliore's essay originally appeared in Eric O. Springsted, ed. *Spirituality and Theology: Essays in Honor of Diogenes Allen* (Louisville, Ky.: Westminster John Knox Press, 1998): 112–23.